STUPID IS AS STUPID DOES

The School Of Hard Knocks

(Book II of I Need God Cause I'm Stupid)

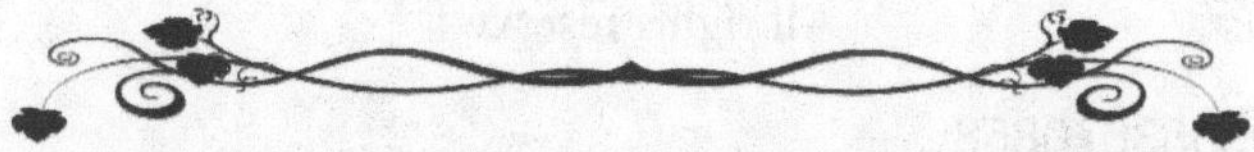

Dr. Michael H Yeager

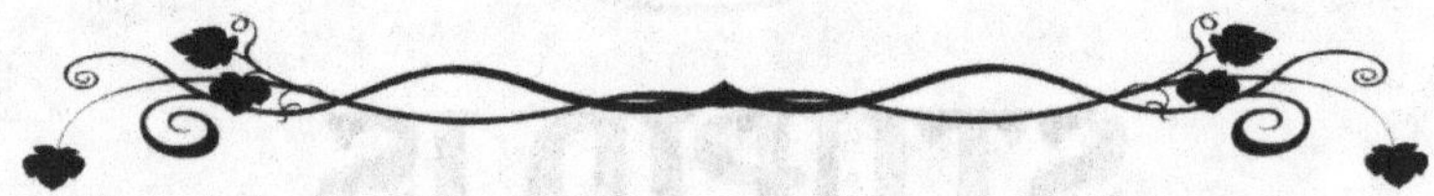

Many of the Names of Those Mentioned in These Books Have Been Changed to Protect the Innocent and the Guilty!

ISBN: 9798353670858
Imprint: Independently published

DEDICATION

These are teachings and experiences are from **Dr Michael H Yeager.** It is written for those who truly hunger and thirst after all that **God** has made available through the life, ministry, sufferings, death and resurrection of **Jesus Christ**. My prayer is that not only will your life be touched by these **divine Truths**, and **Experiences** but you yourself will truly step in to the truth that sets men free. May you experience wisdom, **Transformation**, divine healings, and miracles from the hand of **God**.

LIST OF STORIES IN: STUPID IS AS STUPID DOES

CHAPTER ONE - 8 stories
STOP PREACHING AT YOUR MOTHER
My Dad's Bitterness Deep within Me
Busted up taking bike down Snow Hill
Found out Santa Was Not Real
Alcoholism a generational curse
Drunk at a Catholic Wedding
Transferred to the Public School
Weeds Sprang Up Overnight

CHAPTER TWO - 14 stories
Shot a Trout with a 12 gauge shotgun
Young Girls Prayers Saved Me
Claire's Dads Mind Gone
Spitting on Electric Fence
Downed 1/3 of a Quart of Vodka
Going to Fly like a Bird
Drowning in My Own Vomit
Playing dare devil with a train
Baby Skunks Do Not Spray

EXHORTATION

Dr. Yeager is a man of God who makes errors in judgment. He soars with the Holy Spirit and falls on his face through temptations. Yet, he sings with joy and weeps for forgiveness. He's a man. This book shows how mighty men of God are still imperfect when Satan worms his way into our lives. But joy of joys, redemption, is in Christ. God hears and forgives us when we seek His face and acknowledge our sins, turning away from our sins.

The author shares many fascinating accounts! You feel like you need to hang on to the edge of your seat to brace yourself for what happens next! But, what comes through all the circumstances is a clear picture that God is there to help you even when we do things that are downright, well, stupid.

Doc Yeager: My life experiences along with others that I have had encounters with reveal how easily our hearts go astray, yet God is there. I share many things about HOW I missed God, yet, despite it, JESUS was there. I wrote this book hoping the reader may see the:

#1 Hidden dangers, traps, and snares of the enemy.

#2 That there is hope even in the most hopeless situation.

#3 We are easily led astray, desperately needing to depend upon God for every decision.

#4 That if we repent, cry out to God, asking for MERCY, He will hear our feeble cries and rescue us.

#5 That there are consequences to all of our decisions even though we are forgiven.

#6 If we truly are God's people, the Lord will put us into a melting pot, turn up the heat and cause all of the impurities to come to the surface. Once they manifest, it is up to us what we do with them.

#7 That your heart will even be tested and revealed in the reading of this book!

CHAPTER ONE
REVIEWS FROM THE FIRST BOOK
I Need God Cause I'm Stupid.

Before we get into the nitty gritty, I thought it would be important for you to understand what this book can do for you. First, I never imagined that I would be writing a second book along the same line, But my daughter said to me the other day: Dad it is important for people to understand The dumb decisions that people make in their lives, And the impact of them. She told me: Dad I think you really need to write that second book because it will give understanding, wisdom and hope to people who have made and are making dumb decisions. These reviews are from people who have read my first book and how it affected them.

<u>**Amazon Customer**</u>
Men of God are not perfect.
Dr. Yeager is a man of God. He makes errors in judgement. He soars with the Holy Spirit. He falls, face first through temptations. He sings with joy and weeps for forgiveness. He's a man. This book shows how mighty men of God are still imperfect when Satan worms his way around us. But joy of joys, redemption, is in Christ. God hears and forgives us when we seek His face and acknowledge our sins. This book has shown me these truths and revealed how cunning the devil is, and how merciful my God is. Thank you for this inspiring book. Funny, insightful and real. This man believes so strongly on the WORD!! I love his faith!

Juanita
What a roller coaster
The author shares so many fascinating accounts! You feel like you need to hang on to the edge of your seat to brace yourself for what happens next! What comes through all of the circumstances is a clear picture that God is in control even when we do things that are down right, well, stupid. Great read.

Sylvie
Fascinating and enjoyable
How the Lord looks after Michael is astonishing...at times difficult to believe but extremely fascinating. I look forward to reading more of his works.
Helpful

John Murphy
This is a wonderful book about the Grace and Mercy of the Lord!!! Very inspiring and uplifting let you know that He has said "I will never leave you nor forsake you" EVEN in our own stupidity!!! To God be the Glory!!!

Clara Rodriguez
This was a very interested book gave me a lot hope for my walk that I would love to have with Jesus christ

Elisabeth
Really touching and interesting. Good read/
Helpful

Pastor Frasier
I wish more pastors would be this willing to share!
I have been in the ministry for 30 years and I have met a ton of ministers. They have all had their fair share of mistakes. But, you will never hear them talk about their failures. However, peoples failures are all through the Bible. If people would share how the missed God more, then it would encourage others that God will come though even when we do make a mistake.

STUPID IS AS STUPID DOES

The phrase **"stupid is as stupid does"** is a variation of an older phrase that says **"handsome is as handsome does."** The latter phrase first appeared in writing in 1862. The phrase **"stupid is as stupid does"** became popular in 1994 when the film Forrest Gump was released and has been widely used since.

Proverbs 14:12 There is a way which seemeth right unto a man, but the end thereof are the ways of death.

Stupid Is As Stupid Does: What Does this Funny Idiom Mean?

The phrase "stupid is as stupid does" is a phrase you may hear or see often in conversation and writing. In this book you will find the meaning of this phrase and how you can learn from my Mistakes for you do not have to experience the same tragedies and repercussions.

Some Learning From Mistakes Quotes

As Eleanor Roosevelt
"Learn from the mistakes of others. You can't live long enough to make them all yourself."

Henry Ford
Lessons in life will be repeated until they are learned. The only real mistake is the one from which we learn nothing.

Dale Carnegie
The successful man will profit from his mistakes and try again in a different way.

Leon Brown
Mistakes are the stepping stones to wisdom, we learn from trial & error, we become wise by understanding problems.

Walt Disney

The past can hurt. But the way I see it, you can either run from it, or learn from it.

Robert Kiyosaki

It's not who was right or who was wrong when a mistake was made. It's about who learned from it.

Theodore Roosevelt

The only man who makes no mistakes is the man who never does anything. Do not be afraid to make mistakes providing you do not make the same one twice.

Malcolm Forbes

Failure is success if we learn from it.

Michael Phelps

Things won't go perfect. It's all about how you adapt from those things and learn from mistakes.

Donald Trump

Always try to learn from other people's mistakes, not your own- it is much cheaper that way!

Ron Carpenter Jr.

"A teachable spirit and a humbleness to admit your ignorance or your mistake will save you a lot of pain. However, if you're a person who knows it all, then you've got a lot of heavy-hearted experiences coming your way."

Richelle E. Goodrich

"Many times what we perceive as an error or failure is actually a gift. And eventually we find that lessons learned from that discouraging experience prove to be of great worth."

Kilroy J. Oldster

"Using reason without applying it to experience only leads to theoretical illusions. Ideas derived from real world experiences lead to acquisition of knowledge, and the accumulation of time-tested principles leads to wisdom."

<u>**Sebastien Richard**</u>
"Leadership is all about making the jump, taking risks, and learning from your mistakes. It's about falling, dusting ourselves off, and getting back up again and again and again."

Let The Stories Begin
THESE STORIES ALSO INCLUDE STUPID THINGS I HAVE SEEN PEOPLE DO!

<u>This Book is the School of Hard Knocks</u>

Before I share with you my many Adventures my family and I have experienced, let's look at the scriptures. As human beings, we are all subject to personal stupidity. Sheep are not very smart at all. I could do a whole book alone on the stupidity of sheep. At one time we had a petting zoo. In this petting zoo we had close to a dozen sheep. Sheep by nature are not smart. That is why God uses them as an illustration, as an example of the believer. Sheep need a shepherd.

They need someone to lead them, guide them, protect them, provide for them, deliver them and help them survive. Jesus boldly declared that he was the Shepherd of the sheep. Christ Jesus is the brains of the outfit. Throughout eternity, He and He alone will lead us and guide us.

He is the Vine and we are the dumb branches. (Do we realize that Adam and his wife were sheep before they ever transgressed and sinned against God? Man was created with the absolute need for a shepherd.) Have you ever seen professionally trained sheep?

Men have trained all kinds of animals: dogs, cats, elephants, bears, tigers, etc. The list of animals that men have trained are endless, but do you know one thing we have not seen? Sheep. Do you know why? Because sheep are known to be extremely stupid.

They are the only domesticated animal that cannot live in the wild. Dogs, cats, horses, pigs, birds; almost all domestic animals can live in the wild on their own. Why not sheep? Because sheep need a shepherd!

Now please, do not be offended by this statement. I am not demeaning you or myself. These are simply the facts. Jesus said that without him we can do nothing. That is, anything that is worthy speaking about. That is, anything that the Father can take pleasure in. We desperately need Jesus in every aspect and dimension of our lives. Listen to what scripture teaches us.

book of Psalms:
Psalm 119:71 It is good for me that I have been afflicted; that I might learn thy statutes. **(Read this Scripture again)**

Psalm 119:67 Before I was afflicted I went astray: but now have I kept thy word.   **(Did you hear what the psalmist said)**

Psalm 94:12 Blessed is the man whom thou chastenest, O Lord, and teachest him out of thy law;13 That thou mayest give him rest from the days of adversity, until the pit be digged for the wicked. **(This is a declaration of God working in us)**

STOP PREACHING AT YOUR MOTHER
Doc Yeager 1979

I had led my whole family to the Lord but my mom. I had witnessed to her many times. She had seen the wonderful transformation in my life and I had prayed for her once and her hip had been healed. Not meaning to I began to harp on her, then one day, the Spirit of God arrested me and dealt with my heart that I should just love her and stop preaching to her. We need to understand that we are not and can not change any one. Only God can move upon a human heart to bring about amazing and wonderful change!

We were able to spend a couple of days with my mom in the summer of 1978 since we were passing through Wisconsin on the way to Pennsylvania. She was doing laundry in the basement of her house where the washing machine and dryer were. I went downstairs to help her. As we were doing the laundry together, she started weeping out of nowhere. She was really broken up. I asked her what was wrong. She told me she could not be saved and she was going to hell. I asked, "Mom, what are you saying?"

She replied, "Your father was married previously. He was in the military and had only been married for three months when his wife ran off with another man. He met me many years later when I was only seventeen years old. He proposed to me. I married him and had his children. Your father was Catholic, and I was Lutheran.

He wanted me to become a Catholic, so I went to see the priest. He began to ask questions. When he discovered that I was not your dad's first wife, he said that because my husband had been married previously, I was living in adultery with him. He said that even though his first wife ran off with another man, their marriage was not dissolved; therefore, all our children were bastards. The priest told me that I was going to hell.

All this time I thought that her heart was hardened to the gospel but rather her heart was broken because she did not believe that salvation was available to her. Because she was ignorant of the Scriptures, the devil had her by the throat. I shared with her what Jesus said about this situation and talked about the truth of God's amazing love. She immediately and wholeheartedly gave her heart to Jesus Christ. I held her in my arms as she wept with joy. It was a wonderful conversion.

Romans 10:13For whosoever shall call upon the name of the Lord shall be saved.

My Dad's Bitterness Deep within Me
(Before I was Born Again)

My dad didn't mean to, probably did not even know better, but he was a very bitter man. It was not always evident, but it would come gushing forth out of his mouth and actions. Actually he completely and totally cut me off in the early 90s when he had heard one of my testimony tapes. I simply mentioned that my father had struggled with alcohol and anger. From that moment forward he refused to speak to me again. I did try to reach out to him, but he absolutely refused. I went to go see him one day, but one of my brothers told me that he would shoot me if I came to his property!

People may not realize it but bitterness is contagious. When you have bitterness in your heart, and you begin to share with others who you are offended with. This bitterness has a great possibility of entering into the heart of the person you're sharing it with.

Hebrews 12:14 Follow peace with all men, and holiness, without which no man shall see the Lord: 15 looking diligently lest any man fail of the grace of God; lest any root of bitterness springing up trouble you, and thereby many be defiled;

Bitterness is such a deep, deep hole. Being a pastor since 1977, I have seen many people's lives destroyed and churches because of bitterness that got into a person's heart. The Scriptures strongly warns us about bitterness. One small match of fire in a very dry forest can cause a blazing forest fire that spreads destruction wherever it goes.

I have met people who seem to be angry with me even though they didn't know me. Most of them if they took the time to get to know me, actually changed their minds. You can pretty much tell when somebody does not like you. Through the years as I've had opportunities I have spoken to some of these people. 99% of the time it is because somebody told those people stories about me that were not true. Of course the devil is the accuser of the brethren, and he will not cease his devilish activities until he is finally cast into the lake of fire.

I'm sure there is many reasons why my father was justified in his bitterness, at least in his own mind. The way his father treated him. The way he lost his first wife. The fact that he did not get the credit and the financial rewards he should've from his creativity at the company he worked for. Then the devil fed into his mind that my mother was not faithful to him.

No it is not my plan at all within these memoirs to go into great details regarding many situations. I am not pointing an accusing finger at anybody, because but for the grace of God there I would go. Without Christ within our hearts, rising up within us, we could easily go into the satanic realm of unforgiveness. I hate to think of how many souls of those who confess to know Christ are in hell today because he never dealt with their bitterness.

Almost 50 times in the New Testament it uses the word forgive. Forgiveness is such an intricate part of our lives as Christians. Jesus boldly declared that if we do not forgive, neither will our father in heaven forgive us. Actually the parables teach that if you do not forgive, then all the sins you have ever committed I remitted to you again. This is a very frightening thought. It is actually this truth that has rescued my soul as a believer.

When I saw this Scripture, these truths within the four Gospels, I knew I had to forgive no matter what circumstance or situation that had or has transpired. These truths have kept me in a spirit of meekness, love and forgiveness since 1975.

Until Christ came into my heart, and I discovered his amazing love, mercy and forgiveness, I was controlled and manipulated by the bitterness in my heart. I truly believe that much of the damage I did in my early years, was due to the root of bitterness that came into me as a little child as I heard my father speaking about those he disdained. I'm not blaming my father because I allowed this seed of bitterness to spring up in me.

Busted up taking bike down Snow Hill
1963

You might ask, why are you sharing all of these stories? For a number of reasons. First, it's almost like my own personal journey that I'm reliving as I work my way up to the present. Second, actually I think everybody should share their story, write it down, for their children, and children's children can have some understanding of what transpired in their family. Third, there are definitely lessons, positive and negative that can be learned at someone else's experience.

It was the winter of 1963 with lots of snow on the ground. Now, there was a large field southeast of us were all of us kids used to gather to go tobogganing. It was right next to the graveyard that's in the middle of Mukwonago. There was a deep valley with a large hill. We spent many hours sledding and tobogganing down that hill. We had even built at the bottom of the hill a jump, where we could hit this hill at top speed with our sleds. We would go flying through the air, suspended in space.

One day I decided to ride my bike through the snow. I was going to do something that would impress all of the other kids. I was going to take my bicycle down this toboggan hill and hit the jump. I would fly through the air like Superman, like Evil Knievel on a motorcycle.

From my house to where we went tobogganing was probably only about 1/2 a mile. I finally arrived, and just like I hoped there was a bunch of children there. All of my friends were going to see how amazing I was. I rode my bike across the field to the top of the hill.

It was hard plowing through the snow, but I made it. When it was my turn to go down the hill, I was at the very top looking down. Every eye was upon me. I looked down the hill, and fear began to fill my heart. I thought to myself, this is not a very smart idea. But I knew I had a push my fear aside.

Before I could chicken out, I pushed myself over the edge of the hill. I began to pedal, trying to pick up speed. When I hit that jump I wanted to be really going fast. Faster and faster I went headed for the jump. I could feel every eye of every kid upon me. Here I go.

Then I was there, right at the jump. I hit it going super-fast. And up I went, up, and up, and up. I was flying like Superman. But all of a sudden something happened that I had not planned on. My front wheel started to aim downward like a plane going into a nosedive. And then I was flipping.

I was flipping through the air, head over heels. It seemed like it was forever, but then I hit the ground extremely hard. When my bike hit the ground my face was between the handlebars and the brake handle. It slammed into my face sending stars buzzing through my head. I felt my face being torn. Somehow a sharp part of the break had hit underneath my chin and ripped a large cut across the bottom of my chin to my throat.

I found myself lying in the snow full of pain, blood flowing everywhere. Now, none of the kids ran to help me. They saw Mikey Yeager laying in the snow covered in blood. Eventually, I was able to get up, putting my hand over where I had been cut. Crying and weeping full of pain. Trying to make my way home that half a mile, hurting, bleeding, and trying to handle my bike all at the same time.

Well, that incident caused some stitches right on my chin almost to my throat. For years this scar was evident, but eventually, most of it disappeared. Did you learn anything Mike? Yes, the same lesson over and over. Stupid is, As Stupid Does!

I Was Devastated When I Found out That Santa Was Not Real
1964

There have been intense studies on when children discover that Santa is not real. They believe it is right around the years of 7 to 8. Now, in our situation, my parents went out of their way to make sure we believed in this fictitious character by the name of Santa Claus. Of course, as grownups we know there was a man by the name of St. Nicholas who did wonderful deeds.

St. Nicholas was born in Patara, a land that is part of present-day Turkey, circa 280. He was a Christian bishop who helped the needy. After his death, the legend of his gift-giving grew. St. Nicholas transformed into the legendary character called Santa Claus, who brings Christmas presents to children around the world.

For years a debate has raged over whether parents should **LIE** to their children about the existence of Santa Claus. Some suggest that the years of deliberate fibbing degrades a sense of trust children have in their parents, and the results of a new survey do back up that conclusion. A third of the respondents confirmed they were very upset upon discovering Santa wasn't real and it negatively affected their trust in their parents.

My mom and dad would put cookies out the night before. Then in the morning, they were all gone. They would constantly talk about Santa Claus is going to be here, and you better behave yourself or you will not get anything for Christmas. Christmas was a big time in our home.

I was so enamored by it that I would go out of my way to decorate everything. Actually, I became the number one decorator. Christmas just could not come soon enough for me. I still remember using my dad's ladder to hang the Christmas tree lights on our large popular tree in the front yard. I would hang lights on our rain gutters around the front. Putting lights up around the windows.

I remember one time that we were so excited about our gifts that my sister Debbie and I got up early. Nobody else was up yet. In our excitement, we began to open up the presents. At some time later we realized that we were in trouble. We scrambled looking for tape everywhere. The only tape we could find was a wide black electrical tape that my dad used in his workshop. So we took that black electrical tape and tried to put the wrapping paper on the packages.

It was the most hideous thing that you ever saw when we were done. I still remember seeing these packages under the tree. What's amazing is that when my parents got up with my older brother, no one said a word about the black electrical tape on the Christmas packages.

I think it was when I was eight years old that I discovered Santa Claus was not a real living person. That he did not have a sleigh with eight flying reindeer. There was no North Pole. He did not know when I was naughty or nice. It was all nothing but a big fat lie that my parents had propagated to me.

I still remember to this day getting alone by myself and literally weeping. For some reason, Santa Claus was bigger than life to me. It could be that from this time forward I began to go downhill. I'm not trying to blame this on my parents, but it was devastating. How could Santa Claus not be real? I had literally seen him in a movie called Miracle on Fourth Street. This was a black and white movie made in 1947. Santa Claus had to be real because I saw it in the movie. But No, it was all nothing but a big fat lie. We teach our children these lies and then we wonder why when they get older they do not have any faith in God.

When my wife and I raised our children we did tell them about the real Santa Claus, and who he really was. We told them he was just a make-believe person that people like to imagine that brings gifts for under the tree. We also told them that other people actually told their children that he was real. And that we did not want our children to talk about Santa Claus to their friends less they ruined their make-believe world.

We raised our children with the full reality of Jesus Christ. That the reason for the season is the birth of Jesus Christ, the Lamb of God who came to take away the sins of the world.

Thank God our children were never devastated like a third of the children in America are when they discover the truth!

Alcoholism a generational curse

In my opinion, **alcohol is one of the greatest enemies of mankind**. The famous preacher **Billie Sunday** I believe said it the best.

Sunday said 'I am the sworn, eternal and uncompromising enemy of the liquor traffic. I have been, and will go on, fighting that damnable, dirty, rotten business with all the power at my command.' □ Sunday preached that 'whiskey and beer are all right in their place, but their place is in hell.

Being raised in a family where drinking was the accepted practice, I can tell you that it brought much misery and destruction. My dad's father was a heavy drinker. My dad was a heavy drinker and I do not even want to think about all the money that was spent on that wicked and file substance. But for God's mercy, goodness, long-suffering I would've been dead many times driving under the influence.

There are times when I begin drinking early on Saturday and wake up Sunday morning laying on somebody's floor, not knowing what I had done the night before. Not even knowing what happened to my car. Anybody who drinks to the point of getting drunk knows the mood swings you go through.

One minute my dad was all lovey-dovey, caring and concerned, then the next minute he was a raging maniac. And my mom would say: it's the alcohol talking through him. I have known many people's lives that have been destroyed because of alcohol. All of us children were pulled into this terrible lifestyle. By the time I reached my 19th birthday, I was an alcoholic. Now, it was not just alcohol with me but drugs were also a part of this disastrous lifestyle. Ripple wine, tequila, vodka, Southern comfort, and beer was the order of the day.

Every year, about 88,000 persons die from alcohol-related issues. In 2009, alcohol-induced liver disease was the reason behind 1 in 3 liver transplants. 696,000 students in the college who age between 18 & 24 years get involved in alcohol-related assaults yearly. Likewise, 97,000 students in the college between the ages of 18 & 24 years' experience alcohol-related assault or rape during dates.

Drunk at a Catholic Wedding

It's been so many years that some of these events that transpired are a little difficult to get them exactly right. I believe the first time I was completely and overwhelmingly intoxicated with alcohol was when I was **seven years old**. We were at one of my cousin's weddings, the Hooper's.

Now, my mother was a Lutheran and so was her sister Joan. But both of their husbands, my dad, and Aunt Joan's husband were Catholics. One thing when it came to Catholic weddings in my family was that for sure there was Lots, and lots of booze. Quarter barrels of beer for sure. Now, I have been drunk more than one time at these weddings, and sorry to say did shameful things which I'm not proud of.

But I still remember that night when I was sneaking beer. It's not as if they handed me the beer, but I snuck it off of the tables. Everybody was having a pretty good time, so they didn't really notice me doing this. But they sure knew I had been drinking before the night was over. It didn't take very long before I was completely and absolutely drunk out of my mind. If you can imagine a seven-year-old boy stumbling, falling down, laughing, and eventually I began to throw up to the point of dry heaves.

I was so drunk that night that I do not remember when my parents got me into the car. Or when they tucked me into bed. Or how I got home. Or when I got home. All I remember is waking up the next morning with a splitting headache. From that moment forward I began to drink whenever I could get access to the booze.

When I was 14 years old, I would come home from school and I would open up the refrigerator and take out a Pabst blue ribbon beer. Then I would watch Gilligan's Island drinking beer.

One thing is for sure my dad did not mind me drinking beer as long as I did not smoke dope or pop pills.

Thank God on my 19th birthday, Jesus completely set me free from the evils of alcoholism. As a Pastor I have seen many lives destroyed because of alcohol. People who confess to know Christ but who are slaves of this evil and not even recognizing how destructive it is. Wives being beat when there saved husbands got drunk.

Many of my friends from my old life are dead now because of alcohol. Car accidents, drownings, even suffocating in their own vomit. Let me make this declaration **LOUD** and **CLEAR**-alcohol is **evil, evil, evil**. Avoided it at all cost.

Transferred to the Public School

In the fourth grade my parents had to transfer me to the Clarendon Avenue Elementary. If I understand correctly St. James Catholic School would not allow us to continue to attend. I know it had something to do with money. Not quite sure if it's because my dad did not donate to the church or could not meet the cost of the tuition.

This was a very emotional and drastic event in my life. At least in the Catholic school the nuns did everything they could to stop students from intimidating each other, or making fun of each other.

Now I had stepped into an environment where felt like I was surrounded by nothing but cannibalistic children. Because of my hearing problems, and my speech impediment, the harassment was endless. This caused me to withdraw even more into a shell. Also the public school system brought my brother Dennis and my sister Debbie into the drug world. Debbie was three grades ahead of me, and Dennis was four grades.

Their introduction to the public school system was the junior high school and high school students. This constant harassment eventually caused me to leave school when I was 15 years old, right before my 16th birthday.

The Wickedness of Public Education: Come Out of Her My People

I did not write this book as an attack upon the public school, or secular, liberal, Colleges. It is a wake-up call to God's people. To our great shame as believers in Christ, we are losing our next generation by allowing nonbelievers to do that which is meant to be our responsibility.

Proverbs 22:6 Train up a child in the way he should go: and when he is old, he will not depart from it.
When we bring children into this world, we are given a grave responsibility. Every child has an eternal soul. The destiny of that soul is within the hands of the parents to a great extent. The public education system is never going to train our children to

fulfill the first and greatest commandment.

Matthew 22:37 Jesus said unto him, Thou shalt love the Lord thy God with all thy heart, and with all thy soul, and with all thy mind.

This book will explore many areas where believers are and have been deceived when it comes to the will of God for their children. It is time for God's people to REPENT and to stop sacrificing their children to the devils of this wicked world.

Doc has published over 170 books. Pioneered a K to 12 Christian School, and established a Bible College. He has produced and posted thousands of video Messages on the Internet. Doc Yeager also has written over 5000 sermon outlines on over 30 different subject matters of the Bible. He has preached over 10,000 times. Having memorized a third of the New Testament! Earned a Ph.D. in Biblical Theology, and received a conferred Doctorate of Divinity from Life Christian University.

https://www.amazon.com/dp/B09BG3F27V

Weeds Sprang Up Overnight
1966
Your Weeds will find you out!

Galatians 6:6 Let him that is taught in the word communicate unto him that teacheth in all good things. 7 Be not deceived; God is not mocked: for whatsoever a man soweth, that shall he also reap. 8 For he that soweth to his flesh shall of the flesh reap corruption; but he that soweth to the Spirit shall of the Spirit reap life everlasting.

My dad always planted a garden in the back yard of our house. If there's anything I hated, even to this day it was working in a garden. He would make us kids go out to pull the weeds.

I remember one particular summer day when I was going to go

fishing with my buddies. My dad told me that I could not go fishing until I had pulled every weed in his garden. He was headed off to go to work early in the morning. So, I am stuck at home working in the garden while my friends were having a good time fishing.

As I was pulling the weeds of thought came into my mind. This was too hard of work, I had to find a way to cheat the system. And it came to me in a flash of brilliance. I ran into the kitchen of our house. Opened up one of the cupboard drawers, and right there was my answer. A small butcher knife.

I ran back outside and got down on my knees. I took that little knife and shoved it down into the dirt next to a weed. Lickety-split the weed pulled right out. Of course, the roots did not come out with it. But who cared, because there were no weeds above ground. For the next hour, I worked fast and furious in order to take care of all the weeds. My buddies were fishing and I was missing the fun.

Before I knew it, the garden was done. I gathered all the weeds into my little red wagon and pulled it over to the brush pile. I made sure to cover-up the weeds from my dad could not see that none of them had any roots.

I had no concept of the truth that says *Your Sins Will Find You out! I went on my way fishing. Later that night when my dad came home, he walked out to the garden. I think it was one of the only times I ever heard my dad complement me. He told me that he was proud of the wonderful job I had done. There was not one weed in the garden.

In Galatians, there is a Scripture that says: be not deceived, God is not mocked. That whatever a man sows he will reap. He that sows to the flesh, will of the flesh reap corruption. But he that sows to the Spirit, shall of the spirit reap life everlasting.

For a couple days it looked like I had gotten away with my sin. But almost overnight these weeds sprang back up, faster and bigger than before. My dad immediately notices that something strange was happening. How could those weeds come back so fast, and even bigger than before? He got curious to my detriment. He went to the brush pile and began to shove his way through the weeds. He found all of the weeds I had taken a butcher knife to.

The next thing I knew he was dragging me out to the garden. He pointed to all of the weeds in the garden, and then he held up the weeds in his hand. He showed me the weeds with no roots, and I knew that my goose was cooked. Believe me, the punishment was much worse than if I would simply have done what was right.

Your Weeds Will Find You Out.

CHAPTER TWO
Shot a Trout with a 12 gauge shotgun
1968

I went hunting one day with a friend of mine, Pete Peterson by name. He lived on a farm that was north of where my house was in Mukwonago. I was approximately 12 years old. As we were hunting, he went one way, and I went another way.

I had the 12 gauge shotgun with me that my father had let me use about a year before.

That was the time when I was leaning on it during the heat of the day when something knocked my hat off from the back of my head. As I leaned forward, there was a branch in the trigger of the gun, and it went off. If I had just moved a little bit previous to this, the deer slug would have cut me in half. God had been watching over me and save me from my stupidity.

I had not seen any deer that whole morning. I did have a deer slug in the gun as I was walking over a rather wide creek. I look down in through the clear ice.

Stupid Is As Stupid Does

I saw a huge rainbow trout underneath the ice at my feet, which was swimming up against the flow of the water.

In my excitement, I took my 12 gauge gun without thinking. I put the barrel almost directly to the ice, and I pulled the trigger. Of course, there was an explosion of ice everywhere, and the sound of the gun produced a massive boom. When everything cleared away, I looked, and to my amazement, the concussion of the slug going through the ice had caused the rainbow trout to be shocked.

I took the glove off of my right hand and fell to my knees. I Put the gun down, then reached my hand under the ice into the water and grabbed this huge rainbow trout that was stunned. That night we had a tasty rainbow trout instead of deer venison.

Three People Died In Front Of Us

One day, my mom plus a neighbor lady plus one of my friends and I were headed out to the Flint locks. They were going to drop us off for we could go hunting. On the way, there was an old truck that passed us like a speeding bullet. It went past us very fast. About, a mile down the road, we came upon a very terrible automobile accident.

That very truck that had passed us had lost control and slammed into a telephone pole. The vehicle had hit the telephone pole so hard that it had snapped in half.

The telephone pole had brought that vehicle to a crashing halt. My friend and I immediately jumped out of my mom's car to see if we could help the people in the truck. We ran up to the side of the vehicle and what a horrible sight that we saw.

As I looked through the side window, the very first thing I saw was that there were three people in the truck. And none of them had their seatbelts on. On the passenger side where I was standing, there was a man who was probably in his late twenties. The glove compartment had come open, and when the truck had hit the telephone pole, the steel glove box door, the lid had opened up.

The 20-year-old man because he had no seatbelt on was throwing forward. The lid of the glove box had ripped his guts out. So this young man was sitting with his innards in his lap. Not only that, but his face had gone through the windshield.

The windshield was not the type that crumbled into pieces. The vehicle was too old for that style of the windshield. The windshield was nothing but a mass of shattered slivers of glass. And when his face went through the windshield and came back, it had taken off about half of his face.

Now the man who was driving was an older gentleman probably in his 50s. The steering wheel had come back and gone into his chest. I noticed right away that one of his legs must have been a fake leg for, it was completely ripped off and it was laying there.

His face had also gone through the windshield and was ripped into pieces. But the most terrible thing that I saw that day was a little boy who might've been between six to seven years old in between the young and the old man.

He must have been standing in between but look to be his grandfather and his father and when they slammed into the telephone pole. The little boy had gone through the windshield, and he had been thrown back, once the vehicle had come to a stop. His head was laying back over the front seats, and blood was gurgling out of his mouth.

My friend and I stood there, helpless. We didn't know what to do because it was such a bloody mess. During that time, a woman came running out of the house screaming, and she must have known these three people because of what came out of her mouth.

I can still remember her screaming, Tommy, Tommy, Tommy, as she ran to the car, hysterical, weeping and crying. My friend and I stood there, not knowing what to do. Finally, the ambulance and the police came, and we walked away. From what I understand, all three of those people died. That was my first introduction to a gruesome death.

This also created within me an understanding of why we should always wear our seatbelts.

Young Girls Prayers Saved Me from Going to Hell
(2016)   (9 years later she became my Wife!)

As I share this experience, tears are filling my eyes. May this story help you to never underestimate what God can do when you pray! One day, not too long ago, I was in the sanctuary of the church I pastor praying. I was walking back and forth in the very front, by the altar. My heart was filled with overwhelming thankfulness and gratefulness for God saving my wretched and miserable soul. You see at one time I was extremely lost, in bondage to drugs, alcohol, and immorality.

On my 19th birthday, February 18, 1975, at about 3 o'clock in the afternoon I was in the process of committing suicide. I was a manic depressant and simply wanted to die. I had a large survival knife that I was using, getting ready to cut my wrist. As I was weeping full of self-pity, with the sharp blade pressed up against my wrist, something supernatural and amazing happened to me.

A blanket of God's divine fear fell upon my heart. At that very moment, I knew that I knew that I deserved hell, and I was headed there. This reality was so real that it shook me be to my innermost being. I dropped the knife into the sink and fell to my knees crying out to Jesus Christ in prayer. At that very instant, I was gloriously born again. Jesus set me free from the drugs, alcohol, perversions, depression, tobacco, worldly music all at one time.

Now here I was, over 40 years later thanking God for my glorious and amazing salvation. **All those years I had shared with people about my salvation experience, telling them as far as I knew my salvation was a SOVEREIGN move of God.** I had not known any believers or anyone who had been praying for me. In my heart, I always assumed that it was simply that God had a plan for me. That God had simply by his sovereign will, and his mercy stepped into my life, snatched me out of the hands of the enemy, saved my soul, and put me into the ministry. It is so easily and it comes naturally to assume certain things in life!

As I had my hands lifted towards heaven praising God that I was rescued from a life sin and perversion, I had an open vision.

Now, an open vision is one in which your eyes are open, but you see into another realm. To share with you exactly how this works would take too long. I suggest you get my book called "How God Leads and Guides".

In this open vision, I saw this slender young girl who was approximately 10 years old. She had long blonde, strawberry colored hair. I saw this young girl standing with her hands reached out to heaven. The vision almost seemed a little grainy like it was from an old movie back in the 60s. This vision was so realistic that it almost took away my breath. This is how God moves. One moment everything is normal, and the next minute you're into the supernatural.

This young girl had her hands reached out towards heaven. She was crying out and praying to God for something. And then I heard her prayer. I could hardly believe my ears. She was crying out for her husband to be. She literally was reaching into the future asking God to prepare the man who would be her husband. As I heard her sincere and desperate prayer tears began to roll down my face. It was like the glory of God was shot down upon her. I knew the Lord was hearing her.

1 Peter 3:12 For the eyes of the Lord are over the righteous, and his ears are open unto their prayers:

As I'm standing in the sanctuary of our church with my heart transfixed upon this vision, I said to the Lord: Lord what is this? He said to me: because of her, I was able To Rescue You! I said to the Lord: WHAT? The Lord said to me: It is because of this girl's prayers I was able to save your soul. I stood there in complete shock and amazement. With the trembling lip, I said: Lord who is this? He said to me: This is your wife, Kathleen! She cried out for your soul as a young girl praying for her husband to be.

When I heard, the Lord say this, my heart literally broke. (I'm not exaggerating) I began to weep with a heavy sob. All these years I had assumed that my salvation was based simply on God's sovereignty. He had rescued by soul because He had a wonderful job for me to perform. Now here I was 40 years later discovering that my whole salvation had depended upon a young girl crying out to God for her future husband. Oh, how I wept, and rejoice in the fact that God hears and answers prayers. I had loved my wife before this experience, but not my soul was bursting with new found love for my precious wife of 37 years.

Later that afternoon I went home specifically to see my wife. I said to her with almost a tremble in my voice. Baby doll when you were a young girl, did you cry out to God for your husband to be? She looked at me with utter sincerity. She replied: Yes. She told me that she prayed all the time that God's hand would be upon her husband. She did not tell me exactly what she prayed, but I had heard her praying for her husband in this open vision. I thanked her profusely for her prayers. I believe it is because of her prayers that I am her husband today and a minister of the gospel.

Do not ever doubt for even a moment that God does not hear your prayers. My wife Kathleen reached into the future, and nine years later it rescued my soul. Many times, when I should've died in between those years, God was using her prayers to keep me from dying like many of my friends in the gang I used to run with. Even those years before I got saved there were many times and I was amazed that I did not die in accidents and tomfooleries. Thank You, Jesus, For the Faithful Prayers of your Saints.

Claire's Dads Mind Gone

From the age of 14 up to 17 years old I would stay overnight at the Flintlocks house. One night as I was sleeping upstairs in Clare and Larry's bedroom, somebody came in through the door.

Claire put his finger to his lips and told me to lie still and be quiet. Well, it turned out it was Claire's Dad. He came in with a 12 gauge shotgun. He took this 12 gauge shotgun, and he put the barrel to my head.

I laid there very quietly, not moving or hardly breathing. He stood there with that shotgun set to my head for probably five minutes. Finally, he put the gun down, leaning it up against the wall, and walked out. Claire jumped up out of this bed and turned on the lights. He was in the upper bunk, and I was on the bottom, bunk.

Claire opened up the 12 gauge. It was a single shot, 12 gauge, but in the barrel was not a 12 gauge shell, but a 14 gauge shell.

 Now, if he would have pulled the trigger, it probably would have killed him and me. Claire's dad had almost lost his mind because they had lost two of their children. He also had lost some of his family members, which had greatly affected his mind.

Spitting on Electric Fence
1971

One weekend as I was with the Flintlocks, we had gone to a local party in a little town called Caldwell. We had walked over some of the farmer's fields to get there.

On the way back from drinking, I completely forgot about an electric fence. When we came to the electric fence for some stupid reason, I thought maybe the electric fence had been turned off. So I got this brilliant idea. I knew if I put a little bit of spit on the electric fence that I could hear it sizzle.

So I got down close to the electric fence, and I spit on it. The only problem was that my spittle stuck to my mouth at the same time it hit the fence. When that electricity hit my spittle, it kicked me in the face. I saw red, white, and blue. The next thing I knew, I was waking up laying on my back looking up at the sky!

Downed 1/3 of a Quart of Vodka

We began to increase our drinking, and one day Claire and Larry had been able to get a quart of vodka. We divided it up into three sections. We all decided to Chug the Vodka down as fast as we could. Before I knew it, the third of the quart of mine was gone. I had drunk it all. Well, it hit me like a ton of bricks. Claire and Larry left me in the bedroom upstairs.

Going to Fly like a Bird

The Flintlocks house was a large, old farmhouse. They left me upstairs because I was too drunk to go anywhere. They didn't want their parents to see me in my drunken condition. Well, it got into my silly head that I was a bird.

I do not know why this happened; there were no other drugs involved. To It was summertime, and the 2nd-floor window was open, so I crawled up unto the window sill, and I began to shout, I am a bird, I'm a bird, I'm a bird. I'm going to fly. At that moment I went to jump out the window.

Thank God that Claire had heard me and he had come running up the stairs. He had opened up the bedroom door, and there he saw me. I was perched on the window sill like a bird. Well, I went to the jump. He grabbed me by the back of the shirt, and he pulled me back in with my feet hanging over open air.

Drowning in My Own Vomit

Well, when I was brought back in from the window, I laid on the floor and in a little while I passed out. Once again, Claire saved my life. I still remember to this day, I woke up choking in my vomit. Here I had passed out, and I had vomited on my back. I was breathing in my vomit! Claire was there to turn me over onto my belly before I suffocated.

 Not realizing as I look back, that this was not as abnormal as I thought it was. Quite a number of people do die every year from their vomit when they pass out. It was probably five years to six years later that Claire, who had saved me from drowning in my vomit by turning me over actually was found dead. They said that he had suffocated in his own vomit.

Drugs and Alcohol

There are several different ways that drug or alcohol use directly or indirectly cause asphyxiation death. One way is through pulmonary aspiration, in which the inhalation of vomit into the lungs directly blocks the flow of oxygen. Unless interventions are made to clear the air passages, a person can literally choke to death on his own vomit.2 Sometimes the aspirated material can get into the lungs leading to pneumonia.

Alcohol, in particular, has a tendency to produce large amounts of liquid vomit. When intoxicated, people are not only less in control of their motor and mental functions, many of their natural reflexes—including the pharyngeal reflex (a.k.a. gag reflex)—are immobilized by the depressive effects of alcohol.3 This was the cause of death for rock legend Jimi Hendrix and Bon Scott, the lead singer of the rock band AC/DC.

According to the research from the National Programme on Substance Abuse Deaths in London, 23% of all overdose deaths are caused by asphyxiation, second only to direct acute overdose (drug poisoning).

Playing dare devil with a train

One day Claire and I were out driving his old Chevy Impala. We were at the top of a tall hill.

The road went steeply down and then it took a sharp turn to the left and went over a set of railroad tracks. As we came up the hill, we could see a train was coming. It was coming from the left direction, and that was the direction we were driving parallel to the tracks.

Claire looked at me, and he said to me, Mike, do you think we can beat that train before it gets over the tracks? I told him, Let's Try. The car did not have a souped-up engine in it. It did have a V-8, but I don't know what size it was. I know it wasn't speedy.

Well, the train was a little bit ahead of us, so Claire gave it all the gas he could coming down the hill. The closer we got to the curve where we were going to have to go over the railroad tracks, the more it looks like there was no way we were going to make it. But we had already committed ourselves to this fool, hardy endeavor.

We came down, and we got to the bottom of the hill, and we came around the curve on almost two wheels! It looked like we were going to run smack dab into the training. Claire had the car going full speed ahead. We made it to the tracks and went up over the tracks.

As we went over the train tracks, the train was so close to our back bumper; it felt like it was going to roll us with the wind. Amazingly miraculously, based upon God's goodness and long suffering we were able to make it across the track without being hit.

Baby Skunks Do Not Spray
1972

A friend of mine and I had gone somewhere to go fishing. As we were coming back fishing, and coming down a backcountry road, we saw a litter of baby skunks. We pulled off the road into the field.

My friend said to me, hey, look it; there are some babies, skunks. I sure wish I could have one. I told him, we'll go ahead and get it. He said, oh no, they will spray me. I told him, no, they're not mature enough at that age to have glands. You can go ahead and grab one, and you won't get sprayed.

So he very eagerly got out of his pickup truck. I stayed in the pickup truck because I knew what was about to happen. He ran over before the baby skunks could scatter. He grabbed one of the baby skunks and as he did it let loose.

 The air was filled with a small cloud as he dropped the skunk. He ran back for the truck, choking as he went. I don't know if he ever forgave me for that day when he was sprayed by that baby skunk.

The ability to spray starts early on in skunks. The spray has an oily appearance, and comes out of scent glands below the animals' tails. ... However, skunks generally are old enough to have their totally realized spraying skills when they're in the ballpark of 3 months old, give or take a couple of weeks.

A Chip off the Old Block

My life began to become extremely dark. When I would go home, I was very disrespectful to my mother. One day she finally got fed up with it, and she said to me, you're just a chip off the old block. She was referring to my dad at that moment.

I took that declaration as a badge, as a prideful statement. Now that I look back, I realize that it was not a good statement at all. I used to brag about how my mom kept the house so clean, and I would encourage my wife to do the same.

One day my mother Shirley heard me upbraiding my wife (Kathleen) for not keeping the house clean.

 My mother took me aside and said to me, Michael, do you know why I kept the house clean? I didn't know what to answer her, so I kept my mouth shut. She said, **Michael if I did not keep the house thoroughly clean, your father would beat me.**

Not all impressions we have as children are correct, and many times they follow us into our adulthood. We need to stop, and we need to consider all that we have embraced, all that we have been taught, all that we have believed.

How Did I Get Home?

A couple of weeks later, I was at another party drinking quite heavily. I still remember the kids were all standing around as I stood next to a boat outside.

We were next to a lake. I drank so much that before I knew what I was doing, I began to vomit in front of everybody. I must have fallen and passed out. I came to laying partly under the boat with everyone gone.

Then everything went black again. The next thing I knew, I was waking up on the floor of the front room of our little box house in Mukwonago. I had no idea how I got there.

I got up off the floor, and fear filled my heart. How in the world did I get from Illinois back to Mukwonago and end up on the floor of our front room? I very timidly walked outside to see if my car was in the driveway. Sure enough, my car was in our driveway.

Somehow, miraculously though I was drunk out of my mind, I had been able to navigate my car home the night before, and I passed out on the floor of the front room of our house. How did that happen? Amazingly I did not get myself killed. Remember, I was still only 16 years old. Was many years later that I discovered it was my future wife's prayers that God was using to keep me alive. God was watching out for me through her prayers.

Just the other day (5/27/2019) my wife told me she would be weeping and praying for her future husband as a 13-year-old girl! Sad to say many do not have someone praying for them!

Playing Russian roulette as Driving 1974

As I was in Wisconsin, on leave from the Navy, I began to hunt and fish again with my old friend Claire. I told him my dad had a cabin up at the Yellow River, which was probably about a four-hour drive, 240 miles.

He suggested that we could stay at the cottage and put a trap line out and hunt at the same time. He had a gold covered 22 six shot revolver. He pulled the bullets out of the chambers and took one of the bullets and took the lead off of the end of the shell.

So all there was left was the cap, the gun shell with the powder still in the cap. As we were driving, we would play Russian roulette. He'd spin the chamber, put the gun to the side of his head, and pull the trigger. Then as I was driving, I did the same.

At the time, we didn't realize that gun powder that was still in that gun, if it would have gone off, would have been enough to blow a hole in the side of our heads.

Not too long ago, I heard this tragic story about a youth pastor who decided to do that as a part of a play in his church.

A minister who was using a gun to compare sin to Russian roulette died after shooting himself in the head with a blank round before several hundred parishioners, including his family.

Melvyn Nurse, 35, died Thursday at University Medical Center, five days after he shot himself during his sermon at Livingway Christian Fellowship Church International.

"I thought it was part of the sermon, that he was supposed to fall. When I got up there, I saw blood on the carpet," said Anthony Speight, the church pastor.

Nurse was preaching about sin and guns when he raised the gun to his head and pulled the trigger, shattering his skull.

During the sermon, Speight said, Nurse opened the gun's cylinder, inserted a blank, spun the cylinder and closed it. Blanks contain a hard cardboard-like wad that shoots several feet from the barrel when fired, police said. Nurse did not realize the blank could injure someone and how dangerous it still was.

God was once again watching over my stupidity and not believe he was answering the prayers of my future wife Kathleen to be.

Roller-skating blues

1975

My mother used to roller-skate in the roller derbies. She was one tough little lady. I remember as a young boy watching those ladies on black and white television fighting it out on the oval skating rinks. My parents bought all of us kids roller skates when we were very young. I remember trying to roller-skate on the rough asphalt roads and sidewalks. My brother Dennis, Sister Debbie and I were all proficient with the skates.

The base in Adak, Alaska where I was stationed in the Navy had a roller-skating rink at the base. I ended up working there for a while as one of the caretakers. I had plenty of time to perfect my skating skills. I was especially good at skating backwards.

My wife still complains and tells me that I wiggle my rear end too much. Actually, I was quite proud of myself and my skating skills. Now, don't misunderstand me. I was not Olympic quality, but I could keep up with quite a number of the best.

Back in those days, I do not remember anyone wearing padding to protect their arms or legs. None of us wore helmets to protect our heads. This was back in 1975. On this one day as I was skating backwards, (there was a rather large crowd there that day) I was going too fast.

When, unexpected, someone behind me (which was in front of me) fell. I could not avoid them. The heels of my skates ran right into their mid-drift. Wow, did I go flying. I mean I was airborne. When I came down, I slammed my right forearm into the hardwood floor with all of the weight of my body. The speed at which I was going impacted my elbow and traumatized my entire forearm.

I knew instantly that I had broken my arm. I cannot remember to this day who, but somebody rushed me to the military hospital. They examined my badly swollen and contused forearm. They ended up putting me through numerous x-rays to get an accurate diagnosis. This is where it gets odd.

Amputate My Arm

I knew instantly that I had broken my arm. I cannot remember to this day who, but somebody rushed me to the military hospital. They examined my badly swollen and contused forearm. They ended up putting me through numerous x-rays to get an accurate diagnosis. This is where it gets odd. I had broken my arm, yes, but not cross-wise like normal. I had fractured my forearm vertically, longitudinally along the shaft of the long bone. My bone literally was split from my wrist to my elbow, like a banana cut from top to bottom.

They told me that they really did not know what to do for it but that I needed to be hospitalized. During being in the hospital, somehow my arm became infected. I do not know if it was from the IVs which were being fed into my arm or from something else. My arm was not getting better. It seemed to be getting much worse. After approximately 3 days, one of the doctors came into my hospital room with a very serious look on his face and a bad report (I was 18 years old at the time).

He informed me that the infection in my arm was getting worse. He revealed that he had discussed my condition in a meeting with other doctors. They had conclude that if the infection did not respond to antibiotic treatment within a couple of days, they would have no choice but to amputate my right arm. No, seriously, they said that they were going to have to amputate my arm.

After the doctor had left my hospital room, I laid in my bed wondering what I was going to do without my right arm. I started thinking, "Okay, if my mom was here, what would she do for my broken, infected arm?" Then a thought came to me. (I believe this was the spirit of God.) "Hot compresses!" Yes, that's what my mom would do! She would wrap my arm in hot compresses.

So, I immediately got up out of bed, pushing my IV poll

ahead of me to the bathroom. I took one of the hospital's white towels and put it on the side of the sink. I turned on the hot water tap. When it was really hot and steamy, I put the towel under it. Once the towel was saturated, I wrung all of the excess water out of it.

The towel was so hot that I could barely touch it, but I really didn't care. This was a matter of keeping or losing my arm. I then wrapped this hot towel around my swollen right forearm. I can still remember the pain that shot up through my body. But I was desperate! When you're desperate you will do things that you normally would not do. I went back to my bed, letting my arm absorb the heat from this towel.

Once the towel got cool, I repeated the procedure all over again. I kept this up all day long, through the night and into the next day. To make a long story short, in less than three days almost all of the swelling was completely gone. Praise the Lord that God saved my arm and I still have it to this day! It's amazing how God works with us and helps us even when we do not know him!

Matthew 14:14 And Jesus went forth, and saw a great multitude, and was moved with compassion toward them, and he healed their sick.

PS: In my opinion it is absolutely stupid just to give yourself over to the medical world. Yet there are many of those who say they believe that Christ is their healer who do that exact thing. In over 45 years of ministry I have seen many Christians go through disastrous situations because they simply leaned unto the arm of the flesh.

CHAPTER THREE
Drowning in Horse Manure

They did not know what to do with me. So eventually, I ended up at the horse stalls. There were Caribou that were released on Adak many years previous to allow them to breed, and to be hunted. So there was a considerable herd upon Adak, Alaska.

The military had shipped some rugged mountain horses to Adak to be used for hunting Caribou. They would let these horses lose while the hunting season was out of season. When the hunting season came in, they would round up these horses and would have to break them all over again.

Now, they had some old Quonset Huts in which they had built horse stalls. My job was to shovel the manure out of the horse stalls. Right outside one of these huts, there was a sinkhole, that filled with water and I would dump the manure right next to or into this sinkhole.

The sinkhole was probably more horse manure than it was water. One day I got on the back of one of these horses. They allowed me to ride them and to try to help break them to where they would be suitable for riding and hunting. As I was up on the back of one these horses, it began to try to buck me off.

I pulled the reigns back, and it began to go backward. It went backward out of the Quonset hut to where it ended up against the back side of this sinkhole. The horse reared up off of its front hoofs. It ended up standing almost straight up with me on its back.

Before I could do anything about it, it fell backward with me in the saddle. It landed on top of me, shoving me underneath the horse manure and the water, and it began to thrash around. I was underneath the sewage, the horse manure, and the water with the horse on top of me.

It was a miracle that I did not in that very moment die and split hell wide open. But God miraculously somehow got the horse to roll over on its side and claw its way out of the hole. There was nobody there to help me get out of the sinkhole.

I was able to get back to the shore from the sinkhole filled with horse manure and water dragging myself like a wet manure covered rat back to solid ground.

Spiting Tobacco on the Sidewalk
1975

One day, as I was going to the cafeteria, I happened to spit tobacco on the sidewalk. A young ensign saw me do this, and he made me stop and wipe it up. From then on I decided that I would no longer get in trouble for this, so I picked up the habit of spitting the tobacco juice in my left, front pocket. Why? Because I thought I was cool having the tobacco juices overflowing my pocket. Oh, how the foolish and the degenerate wallow in their mire!

I think that you can begin to see what kind of a mess I was. **However, supernaturally one night, God stepped into my life, instantly and radically changing me forever!** My last three months of military life was so amazingly transformed that I was put in charge of working parties and details from time to time. God instantly delivered me from all of my devices including all of my foolish behaviors. I was a new creature in Christ! Christ had supernaturally set me free from the tormenting demonic powers that had possessed my life for so long!

God's presence disappears
God, where are you?

This Little Teaching Could Save Your Life!

In our walk with God, there are many things that we absolutely must learn. I wish that we could instantly learn them just from reading the Bible, but this is not the case. I had to learn a very hard lesson early in my Christian walk that many who have walked with God for years still have not learned. I believe the reason I had to learn this lesson was because of the amount of trials, tests and hardships that I was about to experience throughout my lifetime. I had to learn how to not live by feelings or by the circumstances that surrounded me.

I gave my heart to Christ on February 18th, 1975. The reality of Christ came rushing inside of me like a mighty ocean of life. My whole life before had been filled with pain, sorrow, depression, low self-esteem, physical disabilities, etc. You name it, I had it. But when I gave my heart to Christ, the presence of God instantly overwhelmed me. It was like electricity going through my body 24 hours a day, seven days a week. This did not go away but continued upon me.

I instantly was set free from all addictions as well as my emotional and mental problems. I was a brand-new creation in Christ Jesus. I fell in love with my Lord Head over heels. I immediately began devouring the Word of the Living God, specifically the four Gospels. I got filled with the Holy Ghost, healed and preached my first sermon very shortly after I was saved. I think that I took the presence and the touch of God upon my life for granted at that time, as if that was the normal everyday experience for every believer. I was soon to discover this was not true.

One morning I got up early to pray and to read my Bible as normal, but something was wrong. I had grown used to the very tangible presence and manifestation of God but, to my shock and horror, it was gone. I mean to me personally; the presence of God was gone. Confusion suddenly clouded my heart and my mind. I cried out to God, "Lord, what's wrong. How have I offended you?" I did not hear any answer which was, to me, also very strange. The Lord was constantly speaking to my heart. I examined myself to see if there was something I was doing that was against the will of God. I could not find anything wrong.

I didn't know what else to do and I didn't really have anyone that I could go to at that time who was mature enough to help me. So, I kept reading my bible, kept on praying, worshipping, praising, and sharing Christ as I went along. I went to bed that night with no sense of God's presence.

The next morning, I got up early hoping that His presence had come back, but to my shock and sadness, God was not there. Once again, I went through the torment of examining my heart, crying out to Jesus and following my regular routine throughout the day. I went to bed that night in the same condition. Now, during this whole experience, I did not back off or give up but just kept pressing on.

This went on day after day after day. God just was not there in His tangible presence. Yes, I did get depressed, but I did not give up. I did not stop praying or reading my bible. I never ceased worshiping and praising God. I did not stop sharing my faith with others and telling them the wonderful things Jesus had done for me. I think approximately two weeks went by with me in this spiritual desert —a no man's land— a dark and dry place in my daily walk.

I did not know what was wrong but there was nothing else I could do but to keep pressing in closer. After about two weeks, I went to bed one night praying and talking to God even though he was not answering me in the same way as He did before.

The next morning, I got up early once again and began to pray when, out of the blue, God's presence came rushing in stronger than ever like a mighty wind. It was like a powerful tsunami, a forceful flood of His presence and His Spirit. God's touch was upon me greatly. I began to laugh, to cry and to shout. Oh, it was so good to have God with me again. I said to the Lord when I was finally able to talk, "Lord, where were you?"

There seemed to be a long pause, then He said to me with what seemed to be a bit of amusement in His voice, "I Was Here All along." You were, Lord? Yes, He replied. And then he said something that was to forever change my life. "I was teaching you how to live by faith." He then began to very specifically teach me out of the scriptures that man does not live by bread alone but by every word that comes out of the mouth of God.

I learned that our walk with Him does not depend upon our feelings, emotions, location or circumstance and that many of those who are believers are destroyed by the enemy because they do not understand nor believe this. Even the apostle Paul had to learn how to be content in Christ in whatever condition, trusting God, knowing that He is not a man that He should lie. Christ has said that he would never leave us nor forsake us. We may call upon Christ with a sincere heart knowing that He will be there for us to answer us and to show us great and mighty things which we know not!

Over 40 years has come and gone since I learned this lesson. I now no longer allow the feelings of either His absence or His presence to affect me. Of course, I constantly examine my heart but if I can find nothing wrong, I simply realize that I am flying by instruments, no longer operating by visual flight rules (VFR).

Thank God, as the aviation industry would say, I am SFR rated! There are two sets of regulations governing all aspects of civilian aircraft operations: the first is Instrument flight rules (IFR) and the second is visual flight rules (VFR) defined as flying by sight and sensory input. All Christians are to be rated as (SFR) which would equate to **Spiritual Flight Rules**!

Romans 4:18 Who against hope believed in hope, that he might become the father of many nations; according to that which was spoken, So shall thy seed be.

HE GAVE HIMSELF OVER TO THE DEVIL

My first encounter with a demon possessed man was in 1975. I had only been a Christian for about two months, and I was in the Navy at the time. I was stationed on a military base on Adak,

Alaska. One night (at about 8 pm) I was witnessing in my dormitory room to three men doing a bible study with them.

While sharing biblical truths with these three men, another man entered my room. We called him TJ. This individual had always been very different and strange. He was kind of out there. I had never even spoken to him up to that time, except one night when he showed a nasty movie to the guys in his dorm. I had walked out of his room not being able to handle his level of filth!

When TJ entered my room, he took over my bible study and began to preach some weird off-the-wall things about the devil. He said he was from California where he had been part of a satanic church. He showed us the ends of his fingers in which some of the ends were missing from the first joint out. He told us that he had eaten them for power, and he had drunk human blood at satanic worship services.

As he spoke, there seemed to be an invisible power speaking through him. An evil and demonic darkness descended upon us in my dormitory. A visible demonic power took him over right in front of our eyes, with his eyes filled with a malevolent glow! One of the guys who were in my room, Hussein (who was a Muslim) declared this was too much for him, and left the room. The other two, Bobby and Willie, sat and listened.

I had never encountered anything as sinister and evil as this ever before. I honestly didn't know what to do at that time, so I went downstairs to the barracks right below me. There was a fellow Christian I had the opportunity of working with who lived right below me. After I had given my heart to Jesus Christ, Willie, the cowboy told me that he too was a born again, Spirit-filled Christian.

I had yet to see the evidence of this in Willie's life, but I didn't know where else to go. I went down to his room and knocked on Willie's door. When he opened the door, I explained to him what was happening in my room. I was able to get him to come to my room upstairs.

Willie stepped into my dormitory and stopped. We both saw that TJ was now up on a stool that was made from a log, and he preaching under the power of satanic spirits. At that very moment cowboy Willie turned tail and ran out of my room. I went after him. He told me that he had no idea what to do and that he could not handle this. He left me standing outside by my door alone.

I went back into my room and did the only thing I could, I cried out to Jesus Christ. The minute I cried out looking up towards heaven, I'm telling you that a bright light from heaven shone right through my ceiling. It was a beam of light that was about 3 feet wide, an all glistening bright light, shining upon me. I do not know if anyone else in my room saw this bright light. All I know is the Spirit of God rose up within me, and I was overwhelmed with God's presence.

My mouth was instantly filled with an amazingly powerful and prophetic word from heaven. I began to preach **Jesus Christ** by the power of the spirit! As I began to speak by the spirit, the power of God fell in that room. The next thing I knew was that TJ had dropped to the floor like a rock.

TJ began to squirming just like a snake his body bending and twisting in I an impossible way. There was no fear left in my heart as I watched this demonic activity. There was nothing but a Holy Ghost boldness and divine inspiration flowing through me at that time.

Now during this divine encounter of Heaven both Willie and Bobby had fallen on their knees crying out to Jesus to save them. At the same time they gave their hearts to the Lord, and they were both instantly filled with the Holy Ghost! The next thing I knew I found myself kneeling over the top of TJ as he was squirming like a snake. I placed my hands upon him. Willie and Bobby came over at the same time joining me and laid their hands upon TJ also.

With a voice of authority inspired by the Spirit, I commanded the demons to come out of the man in the Name of Jesus Christ. As God is my witness, we all heard three to five different voices come screaming out of TJ! After the demons were gone it was like TJ breathed a last long breath like that of a dying man, and grew completely still. After a while, he opened up his eyes that were now filled with complete peace. At that very moment, he gave his heart to Jesus Christ. I led him into the baptism of the Holy Ghost. The presence of God overwhelmed all of us as we gave praise and thanks to the Lord. The next Sunday these three men went with me to church.

Compassion for the Lost

I had an experience of going to hell by a supernatural visitation. After this experience, an overpowering love began to possess me! My heart was filled with immense concern for the lost and unsaved. I looked for men up and down the hallways and in the tunnels of our military facility.

One time when I witnessed to a man about the reality of heaven and hell, he basically said he did not want to hear it. God's love was so strong within me I instantly dropped to my knees and wrapped my arms around his legs. **(I was sincere but sincerely wrong to do this)** I begged him to give his heart to Jesus. I did not want to see him lose his soul and spend eternity in hell.

Arrested for Preaching

The compassion of God was flowing in me like a mighty river. It was so strong that an overwhelming desire came upon me to reach as many people as I could at one time. The idea came to me that I could reach more men on that military base if I went to the movie theater we had on the island.

I remember going to the very front row of this movie theater. I sat down shaking and waiting, wondering if what I was about to do was right. I looked at my watch and knew the movie would begin any minute. Just before they started the movie, I stood up on the ledge where the movie screen was attached to the floor.

I stood there shaking for a while, trying to get up enough nerve to open my mouth. The men in the theater began to yell for me to get off the stage and sit down. Instead, I opened my mouth and began to preach. As I preached, I could see the Holy Spirit was beginning to move upon the hearts of the audience.

It wasn't long before the military police showed up to arrest me. It was amazing that they did not take me by force, but instead waited for me to finish. When I finished what the Lord had told me to say, the police told me to come off the stage. The two of them grabbed my arms and dragged me out of the theater.

They arrested me, put me in their military vehicle, and took me to jail. They asked what I was trying to do in the theater. I took the opportunity to share with them how Jesus had radically changed my life by saving my soul. I told them Jesus wanted to do the same for them. They released me without pressing charges.

A Dear John Letter

Before I had met my wife, I had been dating my childhood sweetheart who was my next-door neighbor. I'm ashamed to say that I had a relationship with her before I knew Christ. Mentally and emotionally, she had captured my heart at a time when neither of us were born again. Actually, I discovered years later that she had not been faithful while I was in the Navy, but that is neither here nor there.

We had planned on getting married once I finished my tour in the Navy but three months before the end of my military enlistment, I had a supernatural encounter with Jesus Christ. I was gloriously born again and delivered from all of my disgustingly wicked habits and corrupt lifestyle. I enthusiastically wrote my wife to be what God had gloriously done for me.

It wasn't long before I received her response: a dear John letter basically telling me to hit the road, Jack. She wanted nothing to do with me or my relationship with Christ. That was the best thing that could have happened to me because it liberated me to go all the way for God. But being stupid, I tried on numerous occasions to restart our relationship. Thank God they all failed. If she would have responded I would never had met Kathleen, or fulfilled Gods Divine call upon my life. Plus I would not have the wonderful three sons and daughter!

Baptized in the Bering Sea

After I was born again, stationed on Adak, Alaska, I read within the Bible about water baptism.

A person that after they give their hearts to Christ, they should be water baptized. This is symbolically declaring that you have died to the old life and that you have become alive to a new life.

As I studied this scripture on water baptism, I discovered that they baptized in the name of the Father, the Son, and the Holy Ghost. They also baptized in the name of Jesus.

I went to a preacher that I had met on Adak and asked him if he would baptize me in the Bering Sea. He informed me that there were icebergs and killer whales in our bay! One of the Navy Chiefs and his son were attacked not too long ago in their skiff! Now, this is still in April. I told him I needed to obey Gods command, so he relented to my wish!

So we had a baptismal service where another young man and myself entered into the Bering Sea. I have never experienced water so cold in all of my life.

Remember we're way out there on the Aleutian Islands, and there were icebergs in the water. Not only was their icebergs in the water, but we were in an area where there were many killer whales, seals, and walruses.

The preacher took me out into the water, and as he put me under, I had him pray in the name of the Father, the Son, and the Holy Ghost in Jesus' name. I still remember as I came up out of the water. I was a 19-year-old kid, but I knew the presence of God had utterly engulfed me. I did not even feel the cold of the water or the air that day. All I knew is that I had obeyed the scriptures and had been water baptized in the Bering Sea.

GOD Said: You Better Not Lie or You'll Die!

One day in 1979, I picked up a book by a well-known author. This book had come highly recommended by one of my favorite preachers at that time. The topic was about angelic visitations. This was something I was interested in, because of my many experiences with the supernatural. I began to read this book and noticed immediately that there were experiences he said he had, which did not seem to line up with the Scriptures. I did not want to judge his heart, but we do have the responsibility to examine everything in light of God's Word. If it does not line up with the word of God, then we must reject it, no matter who wrote it.

As I was pondering the stories in this book, the Spirit of the Lord spoke to my heart very strongly. It was as if He was standing right there next to me, speaking audibly. What He spoke to me was rather shocking! The Lord told me that the writer of this book would be dead in three months from a heart attack. I asked the Lord why He was telling me this. He said the stories in the man's book were exaggerated, and that he had opened the door for the devil to steal his life. The Lord warned me that day that if I were ever to do the same thing, judgment would come to me. I did not realize that the Lord would have me to be writing books, many of them filled with my own experiences. Now I know why he spoke this to me, telling me that I better not exaggerate my experiences.

When the Spirit of the Lord spoke this to me, I turned and told my wife. I held the book up and said, in a very quiet whispering, trembling, wavering voice, "Honey, the man who wrote this book will be dead in three months from a heart attack." Plus, I told her why the Lord told me this. I wish I had been wrong. Exactly three months later, the man died from a heart attack. God can speak to us through the positive and the negative circumstances of life. We better take heed to what he is saying.

From 196 up to this present moment we have published over two hundred books. This Divine warning from God has kept me walking the straight and narrow road of truth with no exagerations.

666

My Older Brother's Obsession with 666

My brother and his wife were living in Anchorage, Alaska, and when I got back to Alaska, I went to visit him. I had the privilege of leading my brother to Jesus, and also I had led my sister Debbie to Jesus.

Some years later I had led my brother Dan and then my youngest brother, Billy, to the Lord, but to my dismay, my brother Dennis, instead of going after God by the meditation and the study of the New Testament got wrapped into the doctrines of the mark of the beast, six, six, six, and end time prophecies.

All of these years, I'm sorry to say, I have not seen him grow to a great extent spiritually. He has always been catering to weird doctrines, philosophies, and ideas, what we call eschatology and end time prophecies. Much of this teaching is way more detrimental than beneficial to the development and the maturing of the divine nature of God and the character of God within our hearts and lives.

They Tried to Steam Me Alive

At the time that I was with the Yupik Indians, it did not seem as if I had any results. However, the Word of God never returns void. I have been told by reliable sources that one of the young men I shared Jesus with is now an Assemblies of God pastor in the Dillingham area. When I was there, there was no Christian testimony in the community. But now there is an Assembly of God church right outside of Dillingham, Alaska. Now to the story of how I was almost steamed to death.

Steam baths were introduced to Yupik Indians by Russian fur traders and missionaries. The steam baths I experienced in the Bristol Bay area consisted of a dressing room, combination cooling room, and the hot room with very low ceilings that were only about four feet high. They were covered over with tundra to keep the steam and heat from escaping. These hot rooms were called a maqili or McQay.

The wood stove heater was an oil drum on its side with a chimney. Rocks were piled on top of the oil drum. There was half of a steel barrel full of water in the corner of the room next to the exit. They had about a four-and-a-half-foot long piece of wood with a kitchen pan attached so they could scoop water out of the barrel, stretch the pan over the top of the oil barrel stove and dump it on the rocks. This sent forth a tremendous amount of heat and steam. They packed the barrel full of wood for a steam bath. Steam baths seem to be an area of great pride for the Yupik men.

They told stories about how they would pass out, trying to outdo each other. They were known to have fallen on the rocks and burned to death. They stayed in the steam bath as long as they could and then go outside and roll in the snow or jump in the river. They also had a bench right outside where we would sit with nothing but a washcloth covering our loins.

One day they invited me to take a steam bath with them. On that particular day, there were three young Yupik Indians and an older man who looked like a walrus. The Spirit of the Lord spoke to my heart and told me not to be fearful. They were going to try to steam me out of the maqili /McQay. God said not to be concerned because He was going to reveal Himself to them through this test. When we were all in the McQay and had closed the door, they all stared at me, speaking in their native tongue to one another and laughing. Then they dumped water on the red hot rocks.

The older gentleman had control of the scoop. As he continued to splash water on the rocks, it began to get extremely hot. I had a wet rag which they had given me, along with a pan of water at my feet. I dipped the cloth into the water and put it against my face and nostrils. I bowed my head and prayed quietly in tongues. I could hear the water hissing as more and more water was thrown on the red hot rocks. I could feel their eyes staring at me. The heat was almost unbearable.

The minute I stopped thinking about Jesus and praying, it would feel like I was being steamed alive. Finally, I heard the door of the McQay open and closed three times. At this point, I looked up, and there was only the old Yupik Indian and myself. He smiled at me with a toothless grin. I bowed my head once again and continued to pray, knowing this was going to get extremely difficult.

I knew this was a fight for their souls. I wanted the Spirit of God to reveal Himself to them. They needed to understand this was not a white man's religion, but Jesus is the living God and Savior of all men. All at once I heard a huge splash. The old Yupik Indian threw a whole scoop of water upon the rocks and ran out the door of the McQay.

I panicked. It felt like my flesh was being melted from off my bones. I ran for the door to open it, but either it was locked, or they were holding it shut from the outside. I pounded on the door, and at that instant, the Spirit of the Lord arrested me and told me to go back into prayer.

I fell on my face directly on the wood plank floor and began to speak in tongues. The Spirit of God sent a cool breeze where there was no wind. A cold wind blew over the top of me. After what seemed to be a long time, they let me out. I am sure they never understood how I could have beaten them at their native hobby, or how I survived such tremendous heat. They never did ask me. They stared at me when I came out.

James 1:2 My brethren, count it all joy when ye fall into divers temptations; 3 knowing this, that the trying of your faith worketh patience. 4 But let patience have her perfect work, that ye may be perfect and entire, wanting nothing.

The Restaurant Burned Down

When the fishing season was over with, I had to find another job. The local town had a fire department. I went to them asking them if they needed to hire anybody. They hired me to be a night watchman. My job was to have the vehicles ready to run at any moment. They had an old world war one water truck that to start it; there was a pedal in the floor.

You had to push down on the pedal, which would engage the starter. Now this particular water truck, was a real challenge to keep running.

It just never seemed to want to run. Whenever I was on watch at night, I would work on the vehicles and make sure they were ready for any fire call.

One day when I was off duty, the fire alarm went off in the town, and I ran for the fire department, which was staffed with volunteer people through the day. As I got to the fire department, I noticed that nobody had got there yet for the fire truck. Well, Dillingham only had two restaurants, and one of the restaurants had a fire in the kitchen.

 I opened up the garage door and jumped into the old water truck. Well, to my great dismay, it would not start. It took me probably about a half an hour to get it finally running. By the time I got the water truck to the restaurant, it was too late. It was hopeless. We did what we could, but we ended up with only one restaurant left in town because the second restaurant had burned down.

The Perfect Storm
1975

Now caribou on Adak Island combines the pursuit of one of North America's most exceptional big-game trophies with one of the unique hunting environments in the country. Adak caribou come from a genetic stock that produces huge antlers that would make the average hunter crazy with excitement.

The island itself has no predators, so Adak caribou have little to do besides getting fat and growing huge antlers. To say that Adak caribou are unique is an understatement in the extreme. The caribou were introduced to Adak Island in 1958 and 1959, by the Alaska Department of Fish and Game with approximately 200 caribou to help prevent emergency famine and recreational hunting opportunities for military personnel living there.

Our main transport was a 110-foot military tug boat. This military tugboat was wonderful as long as there were not rough seas. Military tugboats are not made for the open ocean but were designed for the harbors to bring in submarines and large ships. We took this tugboat around the other side of Adak Alaska to where a large caribou herd had been spotted by one of our scouts. Adak Island is an island close to the western extent of the Aleutian Islands in Alaska. The island has a land area of 274.59 square miles, measuring 33.9 miles in length and 22 miles in width, making it the 25th largest island in the United States.

Due to harsh winds, thick cloud cover, and cold temperatures, vegetation is mostly tundra (grasses, mosses, berries, low-lying flowering plants) at lower elevations. There were some huge mountains on Adak, including and in an active volcano. Adak is snow covered the more significant part of the year. Powerful gales occur in all months of the year at Adak with the highest chance from December through March. A peak gust of 125 miles an hour wind occurred at Adak in March 1954.

Our journey to the other side of the island on the tugboat was pretty much uneventful. The hunting was extremely good, with several very large caribou taken. I had an opportunity to shoot some caribou, but simply pass them up not knowing what I would be doing with 400 to 700 pounds of caribou being a single person. After a couple of days of hunting, we all met back at the tugboat to take us back to the main base.

As we headed back out to sea, a forceful wind began to blow contrary to the direction we were going. The waves of the Bering Sea began to buck and roll in a very frightening fashion, and it felt as if we were on a wild bucking horse. It was like the sea had become angry, furious, and hungry for the destruction of our vessel. Humongous waves relentlessly pounded against our military tugboat.

Every which direction are tugboat began to tilt. From front to back, and from side to side. It seemed like as if times are diesel smokestacks were going to hit the Bering Sea from left to right.

The waves felt like battering rams against the hull, slamming violently against every part of the vessel. The waves became so high that we lost sight of the horizon, sharp, cold, and bitter winds howling all around us. The roaring and pounding became so loud that it obliterated all other sounds, even the roaring of our diesel engines struggling to plow its way through the angry sea.

I became violently seasick with all of the other sailors on board. It seemed like even the oldest, and saltiest Navy sailors among us were sick. The captain of the vessel told us to stay off of the deck lest we are swept overboard. Our tugboat had run into what we would call the perfect storm.

I am positive that there was not one man aboard that was not crying out to God for our protection and deliverance from this terrible storm. The trip that should've taken approximately five hours took us all day and night until the next morning. All that day and night, we were being tossed to and fro, and shaking like a mouse in the mouth of a sinister and angry cat.

When we finally pulled into the harbor of our military base, we all were extremely thankful to God that we had made this journey home. I think every one of us knew that it had to be God's divine protection that this tugboat afloat in such overwhelming wind and waves. I think it took me approximately three days to get over the terrible seasickness they had wracked my head and body during this caribou hunt. God is so merciful, loving, and protecting in all of his ways.

Chief Lloyd Old's perspective.

We were coming out of three arm bay in (Adams) 110 ft. Tug boat. Everything was fine until we entered into the Bering seaside of the island where we hit heavy winds and rough seas with 40 to 50 ft. Swells. Everyone on board was being thrown back and forth violently. At one time, the skipper of the tug told me everyone onboard was sick, and he was feeling sick too.

He asked me if I could take the controls of the tug while he went below. I agreed, and he left the helm in my hands. My son Brad told me that he had to go to the bathroom bad, so I told him to hang on to the ladder railing as tight as he could and to come right back.

When he returned, he told me everyone below deck was throwing up or moaning, including the tug boat skipper. I told him to hold onto the grab pipe along the bulkhead, and not let go while we were being tossed about. The waves were breaking over the bow of the 110 ft. Tug boat and rolling along both sides of the ship immersing everything under water.

The skipper did finally return, telling me that he felt better now and took back the controls. I was mainly concerned for my son Brad, and with him getting sick, but I guess God has blessed us both so that we ended up not having motion sickness problems, for that I am very thankful. I remember Mike Yeager telling me that he did not want to go through that ever again, but not much else. Once we rounded the northern point of Adak Island, the sea smoothed out considerably.

CHAPTER FOUR

How Not to Cast Out Devils

As I was visiting in Wisconsin from Alaska, I was informed about a Bible study of charismatic Catholics. I was told that a Catholic priest led this Home Bible study.

I could not find any spirit filled born again, churches in any of the surrounding communities, so I decided to go to this charismatic Catholic Bible study. When I got there, I found out that they were heavily involved in what people call the deliverance ministry.

Now there was a young black man there who was probably about my age. He was getting all of the attention and was saying that he needed to have deliverance. So they set him down in a chair, and they began to try cast devils out of him. My experience of casting out devils was that it should be easy, and was not complicated if you were where you needed to be spiritually.

You did not need to talk to the devils. Matter of fact you did not allow them to say anything. You told them to shut up, and to come out by faith in Christ Jesus and by the authority of God's word. Well, the priest would literally be trying to cast up the devils, and then he would go out, take a cigarette break, and he'd come back in.

So this young black man was surrounded by four or five people, and they were all screaming and yelling and telling the devils to tell them who they were, and then to come out. The priest would come in and join them after his cigarette break. As I stood back and I watched all of this unfold, I knew this was not a group of people that I wanted to be connected with. I walked out the door of that charismatic Catholic gathering to never go back again.

Peter Yannotta

Sad. Unfortunately if you try to get these people to think differently they will rear up at you.

Only the word of God hidden the heart can transform the mind.

I was at a luncheon recently where Pentecostal believers were uplifting a church that 'specialized' in deliverance. The 'gifting' was that they knew how to engage the devils in conversation so they knew what their motives were to cast them out.

I thought to myself: These unclean spirits are minions of the father of lies who came to steal, kill, and destroy; and in whom there is no truth (Jesus' own words); so what is the likely of the unclean lying spirit to be telling the 'experts' anything truthful?

I quietly sat and finished my meal and politely left lest there be an offense; because this is the food they ate and drank and was deeply believed by the 'experts'.

Living in an attic
1976

When I arrived back to Dillingham, winter was coming, and I needed somewhere to stay. I somehow ran into a man who was probably eight to ten years older than me. He told me that he and his partner, another man, (red lights were going off) had a house and that if I wanted to, I could stay in their attic. It turned out that they belonged to a religious group called the Baha'i Faith.

They began to tell me about their strange and terrible beliefs. Well, of course, I boldly began to inform them that I was born again, Holy Ghost spirit filled. I told them that Jesus was the only way. For a very brief time, I slept in their attic until it became evident to me that this was not going to work. So I left their attic and went out into the cold. That's how I ended up on the mud flats living in a deserted tent covered with plywood. That winter it hit below -50 with out the wind chill factor!

The Bahá'í Faith is a FALSE religion

They teach the essential worth of all religions, and the unity and equality of all people.

Established by Bahá'u'lláh in 1863, it initially grew in Persia and parts of the Middle East. It is estimated to have between 5 and 8 million adherents, known as Bahá'ís, spread out into most of the world's countries and territories.

It grew from the mid-19th-century Bábí religion, whose founder (the Báb) taught that God would soon send a prophet in the same way of Jesus or Muhammad. In 1863, after being banished from his native Iran, Bahá'u'lláh (1817–1892) announced that he was this prophet. Following Bahá'u'lláh's death in 1892, the leadership of the religion fell to his son `Abdu'l-Bahá (1844–1921), and later his great-grandson Shoghi Effendi (1897–1957).

Bahá'ís around the world annually elect local, regional, and national Spiritual Assemblies that govern the affairs of the religion, and every five years the members of all National Spiritual Assemblies elect the Universal House of Justice, the nine-member supreme governing institution of the worldwide Bahá'í community, which sits in Haifa, Israel, near the Shrine of the Báb.

The Book Said I Had Demons

So here I was, living on the howling, freezing, lonely Mud Flats of Alaska at 19 years old. (1975) Nobody else was there but me and Jesus. One extremely cold morning, I got up freezing. My mustache was covered with frost from my breath. I was so cold that I knew that I needed to start a fire real quick. What I did next, I knew better, but at the time it didn't concern me.

I had some gasoline which I kept to help start fires. I took an old coffee can and filled it probably half-full. After I had the wood stove full of wood, I threw the gasoline onto the logs. Then I took a match and threw it into the 55-gallon drum. Of course, you know what happened. It exploded, sending fire rushing out of the barrel and engulfing me head to toe! The blast was so huge that it threw me onto my back. Despite my stupidity, God protected me. I had some singed hair on my face and head, but that was the only damage.

What unforgettable and amazing adventures I had during that time of my life! I look back now and am utterly amazed at how God kept me and preserved me during those times. Thank you, Jesus, for Your wonderful protection and mercy!!!

Isaiah 43:2 When thou passest through the waters, I will be with thee; and through the rivers, they shall not overflow thee: when thou walkest through the fire, thou shalt not be burned; neither shall the flame kindle upon thee.

I was still living on the mud flats right outside of Dillingham, Alaska. During this time, I did not know any other true believers. I'm not saying that there weren't any in Dillingham, I'm just saying that I did not know of any. I was striving to live for God. I do not remember how or by whom, but a book came to me. This little book has become famous in the modern-day church dealing with the subject of believers having demons.

As I read this book, it began to tell me that every manifestation of the flesh in my life was because demons possessed me. At the time, I was not very mature in the word of God.

I was hoping that this teaching was correct because then the evil desires within my mind and my flesh were not me but demons. This book said that I needed deliverance; I had to cast them out. I mean, I swallowed this doctrine hook, line, and sinker. (By the way, I am not saying that Christians cannot have demons because I have cast them out of believers through the years.)

So, I began to take authority over these demons in my life, my body, my mind and my emotions that were giving me so many problems and commanding them to come out of me **In Jesus Name**. This book said that every time demons would leave you, it would be manifested by hiccups, burping, or the release of other kinds of gas. I'm not kidding you. So, during this time in my life, every time that I burped, hiccupped, or passed gas; I thought demons were leaving me. LOL--- I am not kidding!

For a while, I believed that I was getting somewhere. I did not know that a born again, a spirit-filled believer could have so many devils, but I was soon to discover that it was all an illusion, a deception —a dead end road. You cannot cast out the flesh.

These works of the flesh kept creeping back into my life every time I turned around no matter how many times, I cast the "demons" out. Or, so I thought. I'm sorry to say that for a very brief time, I became more devil conscious, then Jesus' conscious. This is what this kind of false teaching does. It takes your mind and eyes off Jesus Christ and puts them upon the devil, yourself and manifestations.

I then discovered, by reading the Bible, that the scriptures required me to be transformed by the renewing of my mind (Romans 12:2). I am to take captive every thought and subject it to obedience unto Christ. God also requires me to present my body as a living sacrifice; holy and acceptable unto God.

Romans 12:1I beseech you therefore, brethren, by the mercies of God, that ye present your bodies a living sacrifice, holy, acceptable unto God, which is your reasonable service.2 And be not conformed to this world: but be ye transformed by the renewing of your mind, that ye may prove what is that good, and acceptable, and perfect, will of God.

2 Corinthians 10:3 For though we walk in the flesh, we do not war after the flesh:4 (For the weapons of our warfare are not carnal, but mighty through God to the pulling down of strong holds;)5 Casting down imaginations, and every high thing that exalteth itself against the knowledge of God, and bringing into captivity every thought to the obedience of Christ;

Stupid Is As Stupid Does

I have been given the power of choice. I can choose to submit to God and to resist the devil, knowing that he will flee from me. I am not attacking the whole deliverance ministry because there are demonically oppressed, possessed, and depressed, and obsessed saints. I am simply saying that a lot of our issues are not going to be resolved by a one-time or multiple sessions of commanding the devils to go.

We must seek God, renew our mind, submit to and obey the gospel of the Lord Jesus Christ, resist the devil, take up our cross, and follow Christ! Believe me; I have made tremendous progress by meditating upon God's word night and day. So now when I burp, hiccup, or pass gas; I know that it's not demons. I simply ate something that did not agree with my stomach.

I have discovered that most people who give themselves over to this type of teaching are the tormented people I know.

2 Corinthians 2:11lest, Satan should get an advantage of us: for we are not ignorant of his devices.

Explosion Threw Me out the Door of Tent

So here I was, living on the howling, freezing, lonely Mud Flats. Nobody else was there but me and Jesus. One freezing morning, I got up freezing. My mustache was covered with frost from my breath. I was so cold that I knew that I needed to start a fire quickly.

What I did next, I knew better, but at the time it didn't concern me. I had some gasoline which I kept to help start fires. I took an old coffee can and filled it probably half-full. After I had the wood stove full of wood, I threw the gasoline onto the logs. Then I took a match and threw it into the 55-gallon drum. Of course, you know what happened. It exploded, sending fire rushing out of the barrel and engulfing me head to toe! The blast was so vast that it threw me onto my back. In spite of my stupidity, God protected me. I had some singed hair on my face and head, but that was the only damage.

What unforgettable and amazing adventures I had during that time of my life! I look back now and am utterly amazed at how God kept me and preserved me during those times. Thank you, Jesus, for Your wonderful protection and mercy!!!

Isaiah 43:2 When thou passest through the waters, I will be with thee; and through the rivers, they shall not overflow thee: when thou walkest through the fire, thou shalt not be burned; neither shall the flame kindle upon thee.

Depression Overwhelms Me

Thank God for His wonderful mercy, kindness, and goodness. Even when we fall short, He's still there to help us, protect us and to keep us. There was a brief period in my life after I gave my heart to Christ that I backslid. I was like a yo-yo in my walk with God for maybe two months; messing up, repenting, walking with God, and then messing up again, to start the cycle over.

Everything is a little bit foggy about those days. I had come back to Wisconsin from being in Alaska, doing missionary work with the Yupik Indians in the region of Dillingham. Before I left Alaska, deep depression began to hit me hard. I had experienced a lot of persecution while living with the Yupik Indians.

During that whole time of reaching out and evangelizing, I had no fellowship with other believers. I did not know one other believer, except for the local sheriff, who I had stayed with for a brief period. But now he and his wife had moved away, and I found myself all alone living on the mud flats in what had formally been a tent in the middle of winter.

I still remember laying in my goose down sleeping bag on a wooden platform in that tent. 40 below zero outside with the wind whipping and howling over my little structure. Hoping and believing I would make it through another night. I would wake up in the morning trying to get a fire going in my 30-gallon makeshift wood stove. And then I would have to head out into the snow and walk 3 miles to get to the gas station where I worked. God, in his mercy had kept me alive.

There is no one my age (20 years old) or even close to my age that wanted anything to do with God that I knew of in that pioneer town. Another major problem I had is that I did not have enough of the **Word of God in my heart**. This is the main reason for many believers not being able to get victory over the devil, temptations, test and trials, sickness, and disease.

Kenneth Hagan (a minister used to work for) shares a personal story along this line: he said that he was having tremendous meetings where the power of God was falling. Many people were being touched, healed, laughing, crying, and shouting. And yet despite these amazing meetings, many of these same people were living defeated lives and going back into sin. He asked the Lord: **Why this was happening?**

The Lord said to him that a person can continue to breathe and still die. Breathing is symbolic of the moving of the spirit, but the physical body needs food. It is the same with the spirit and soul of man. It takes the word of God being digested daily in the believer's life to be able to overcome the test, trials, afflictions, and temptations that confront us all.

Psalm 119:11 Thy word have I hid in mine heart, that I might not sin against thee.

Not only did I not have enough of God word in my heart, but I was not attending a good, Spirit-filled, Word church. There was no spirit filled church at that time available in Dillingham, Alaska. (There is now an Assembly of God church there.) I began to go into deep depression out on the mud flats of Alaska.

Now here I was, the middle of winter and 40° below with the wind and the snow whipping around my little wooden shack made from a tent frame. I found myself beginning to dabble back into drugs and alcohol.

Fought a Yupik Indian in a Bar

As depression began to overwhelm me, I began to find myself once again drinking in the local bars. One night I was in a bar, and I was disgusted with myself, angry at myself for beginning to backslid, and I was in a terrible mood. This was the only bar in town that had a dance floor. I had also started to date the owner's daughter, Paula.

Now, there was a young Yupik man who was bigger than me who began to push me around. Well, this anger of being not where I should have been spiritually rose up inside of me. Now, since I had accepted Christ, I had lost any sense of natural fear, and I was not afraid of anything but God. When this man pushed me, anger rose up inside of me, (I wasn't angry at him). Immediately I pounced back at him. Before I knew it, I had him out the door of the bar, and I had him down in the snow. That fight did not last very long, but I was headed for deep, deep trouble.

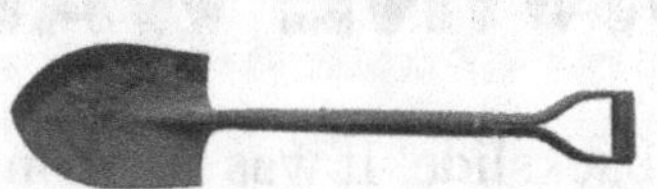

Dad Beats Me over the Head with a Shovel
1976

As I was in Wisconsin, (I was 20 years old) I came home one night to go to sleep. When I went into the backyard of our house, there was my dad, and he was pushing my mom around.

He was extremely drunk at the time. Well, I jumped into the midst of it because I wanted to protect my mom. As I got between him and my mom, uh, he turned away from me, and my mom began to yell at me, telling me that I needed to keep my nose out of their argument.

As my back was to my dad, unbeknownst to me; he had grabbed hold of a short spade shovel. The next thing I knew, my head was ringing. I found myself on my knees as my dad continued to beat me in the head with a short spade shovel. The edge of the shovel must have caught the side of my forehead because blood was running down my face.

As I'm lying on my knees in the dirt, my dad is hitting me with this shovel, and my mom is telling me that I am no longer allowed to live there. Finally, my dad stopped beating me, and I got up, and I walked away. I was kicked out of my parents' house right amid winter with nowhere to live.

A DIVINE WARNING

I had begun to backslide. It was a spasmodic, backslidden condition. I would fall into sin, repent, and get back up. This continued for a couple of months until one night when I had fallen asleep in an almost drunken condition, I had a terrible dream.

While I was asleep, I had this extremely scary and realistic dream. In this dream, it was late at night, and I was coming out of a bar. I was looking at myself as if I was the third person. I could see that I had been drinking by the way that I was stumbling around, falling, and getting back up again. I finally made it to the curb where there was a gutter.

I then fell face down, lying in this dirty, filthy, nasty, sewage gutter. People were walking by me and just staring. None were trying to help me out of the sewage in any way whatsoever. Suddenly, as I'm lying in this filthy gutter, I no longer am looking upon myself as a third person.

I am in my body when suddenly, demonic forces came flooding into me. I mean demons began to enter into my body, and I began to lose complete control as if I had gone into an epileptic seizure. You cannot believe the absolute horror and fear that filled my heart at that moment.

This experience was so real and frightening to me at the time that I immediately woke up sweating and crying. I fell on my knees next to my bed repenting with everything inside of me for giving place to the devil; for returning to sins that I had come out of in which Christ had delivered me.

I knew at that moment that this was a divine warning from God. Scripture says that once a house is clean, the devil will come back to where he had been cast out and if the house where he had been cast out is empty; he will bring back with him seven more spirits worse than himself.

This was the Spirit of God, showing me the reality of where I was headed. Right then and there I knew in my heart that I had to leave my hometown. I had to quit my good paying job and run for my life back to God with everything inside of me. Thank God That That Is Exactly What I Did! Thank God from that time to now I have lived for Christ!

Matthew 12:45Then goeth he, and taketh with himself seven other spirits more wicked than himself, and they enter in and dwell there: and the last state of that man is worse than the first.

Sliding Down the Highway On the Side of my Motor Cycle 1977

I was in Wisconsin for a while longer to earn some money. Wintertime was just beginning to end, and the roads were clear of snow. I took my motorcycle out on the main highway and headed to work in Waukesha, Wisconsin. I was driving approximately fifty miles an hour when tragedy struck. For some reason, I had not noticed that all of the vehicles on the highway were going extremely slow.

It was too late before I realized whhy. The whole highway was covered in nothing but black ice. My motorcycle began to slip out from underneath me; my wheels slid to the right while the top of the motorcycle swayed to the left. At that very moment, I entered a supernatural spiritual realm where everything begins to happen in slow motion. This realm is hard to explain to people. I am not exaggerating when I say time seems to come to a stop.

I had had this experience several times when God divinely intervened on my behalf. I can think of at least ten times this has happened to me.

#1 when a gang leader was trying to kill me by stabbing me to death while coming out of Chicago in his car.

#2 While saving a young man's life from a motorcycle accident.

#3 A large mule deer was going to slam into me on my motorcycle while I was headed through Canada.

#4 My wife and I rolling down a cliff in our car. My newborn son Michael was up in the air, as my wife reaches out and snatches him to her chest.

#5 My seventh-month pregnant wife, my son Michael and I on a 450 custom Honda. Headed for guardrails, telephone pole, and a pile of rocks.

#6 Supernaturally empowered while driving a motorcycle and communist infested lands.

#7 While flying my airplane through a set of high lines.

#8 Right before I slammed my Cadillac into a concrete bridge.

#9 Preventing a young lady from burning to death when her hair caught on fire.

#10 When I was engulfed in a gasoline fire.

Now, as my motorcycle (in slow motion, it seemed to me) slid on its left side, I began to move in rhythm with the falling bike. First I pulled my left foot up out of the way before it was smashed between the road and the bike. As it was falling over, I stepped up over the top of it. At this point, the bike was completely on its side against the asphalt still doing about fifty miles an hour or so. Thank God I had heavy duty crash bars on the front for the driver and the back of the bike for the passenger.

They were designed to protect the rider and passenger but not to be used as skates on ice. Once the motorcycle was completely on its side, it kept on sliding down the road like it was on skates. I sat on it like it was a divine carpet ride. As I was perched on top of the motorcycle, I kept passing up cars.

I slid down the highway, never veering to the left or the right. It was like someone throwing a bowling ball down the middle of the lane for a strike. People were gaping at me as I passed them up. I'm sure they had never seen anything like this in their whole life. The black ice caused there to be very little friction between my crash bars in the highway. There were no sparks screeching of rubbing steel against the asphalt. Eventually, the motorcycle came to a complete stop, lying on its side in the middle of the highway still running.

When the motorcycle had come to a stop entirely, I jumped from it, grabbing its handlebars, and shoving it to its upright position. I remounted my bike, put it in gear (it was still running) and went on my way.

During this whole experience, neither my breathing nor my heart rate increased even for one second. You see, I was no longer backslidden. I was in the perfect will of God. I had peace like a river. The kingdom of God is not in meat or drink, but in Righteousness, Peace, and the joy of the Holy Ghost!

Yes, I did quit my job because my soul was of much higher value to me than the pleasures of this world. I gave them a two-week notice, packed my bags, loaded my little bit of belongings into the saddlebags of my motorcycle, and headed out West. As I drove away from everyone I knew and loved, God once again took hold of my heart. I was on my way and thanked God; I have never looked back!

Philippians 4:7 And the peace of God, which passeth all understanding, shall keep your hearts and minds through Christ Jesus.

Speeding to My Own Destruction

As I went further west, I left behind the flatlands of South Dakota. Small hills began to appear, first one and then another. Eventually, I found myself in the state of Wyoming. While I was in Wyoming, I visited the Yellowstone National Park. After I had spent some time at Yellowstone National Park, I headed west again. I was now entering the foothills of the Rocky Mountains.

As I traveled, I would simply find a secluded spot to camp for the night. As I came into a small logging town one day, I pulled in to a small mom and pop combination grocery store and gas station. I still remember taking my good old time filling the gas tank with gas. At the same time, I was enjoying the fresh country air and the beautiful scenery of the mountains around me. After I drank a small 12 oz. cup of coffee and ate a $.75 hot dog, I climbed back on board my motorcycle.

I have always enjoyed riding bikes. One of the very first bikes I had ever owned was an old antique white 305 Honda dream. I had saved up to buy it with a newspaper route, and working at a strawberry plantation, plus working at local dairy farms. This bike was in beautiful condition for its age.

Stupid Is As Stupid Does

I still remembered with regret how one of my friends begged me to let him take my 305 dreams for a ride. He took it for a ride all right, right into a concrete pillar of a bridge. Larry had overestimated his own ability to be able to go around a corner at a high rate of speed. Larry is seeing that he was not going to be able to keep the bike on the road and that he was going to hit the bridge, leaped off the bike just in time. Larry had survived the accident, but my bike had not. That was many bikes a go.

As I was winding my way through some low-lying mountains, I caught the sound of several high-powered ninja style motorbikes coming up from behind me. In a very short period of time, these motorcyclists had caught up to where I was. They passed me on my right side, with their engines screaming as they sped past. One after another they shot by me on my right-hand side. There were at least five of these ninjas hot dogging it down the road. It was obvious that they were racing one another.

The bikes they were riding were all foreign made, low to the ground, high rpm. Superbikes. These were lean and mean speed machines, designed for racing and taking sharp curves. As they passed me, I could almost feel them challenging me to keep up with them. At that very moment, I was faced with a very crucial decision. I could give into their challenge and go for it, or I could choose to obey the laws of the land, submit to the will of God, resist the devil, and the enemy would have to flee from me.

I'm sorry to say that I gave in to my fleshly desire to go with the crowd. I opened up the throttle of my 750 Honda. It responded with the thrust of a rocket taking off. Now the motorcycle that I was riding was not made for racing but it definitely not a pushover, or kid's plaything. There was a lot of power pumping out of its four cylinders. The only problem was that it was not specifically designed to take the corners like the bikes that I was trying to keep up with.

The heavy-duty crash bars that I had put on my bike, front and back, had saved my life in the last accident. Just about a month before I had flipped it over on its side on the highway when I had hit a patch of black ice. But now in this situation, these crash bars were an extreme detriment.

The crash bars were preventing me from being able to lean into the sharp Corners like I needed to. Normally I would not have been so stupid, but it was as if I had been taken over by demons. The need for speed, and to keep up with these guys was overwhelming. As I gunned my bike to keep up with the other motorcyclist, I could feel the adrenaline pumping through my veins.

I breathed in the familiar overwhelming desire for speed. It was at times like this that it felt almost as if demons had taken me over, and were whispering in my ears. I could almost hear them whispering saying: go faster, faster, faster. I had experienced this before when I had been driving my automobiles or my motorcycle.

Driving like a total madman down the country roads of Wisconsin. It was nothing but a miracle that I had never crashed and died. Close friends of mine had not been so blessed in escaping their tomfoolery. One of my friends hit a tree, and he was so mangled that they had to have a closed-casket funeral. Now here I was again possessed with the need for speed, but now I was saved. Yet even though I was saved this same feeling, desire, compulsion, overwhelming thirst for speed and competition overtook me.

I was barely able to keep up with these motorcyclists. Mile after mile after hair-raising frightening mile I raced after these bikers. With my heart in my throat over and over, I continued to speed up, slow down and suddenly hit my breaks as I came into the corners. As I leaned into these corners, my crash bars would be scraping on the asphalt, front and back. Literally, sparks were flying from my crash bars. But I just would not back off.

The pressure on me to continue to drive like this was overwhelming, frightening, and heart-stopping. My whole body was drenched with sweat. I knew in my heart that it was insanity to be driving in this fashion. This bike was not designed for this kind of driving. Over and over I found myself constantly scraping my crash bars on the asphalt as I went around the sharp corners. Sparks were flying everywhere as the crash bars were meeting the surface of the road.

At times, I was barely able to keep the other riders in my sights. Whoever they were, they were extremely good at what they were doing. Maybe they were Olympian bike riders who were practicing for the Olympics? In 1976, the Summer Olympics were going to be held in Montréal, Canada.

They were also going to be having Motorcycle racing. I know this sounds crazy, but I really do wonder if these motorcyclists had something to do with that. These guys were good and just were not backing off of their speeding or their racing. I could not understand how they could keep up with the speeds they were hitting. Instead of them slowing up, they seemed to be increasing their speed at every opportunity.

I continued to follow them, mile after mile. Now you might be saying: No Way! Yes-way! My nerves were fried, and I was getting very tired and wearied from all of the exertions it was taking for me to keep up with these guys. I knew in my heart that I had lost the edge, I was not responding as I should. Over and over I barely escaped from having a bad accident. These guys were incredible, knowing exactly when to speed up and slow down.

Red lights kept going off inside of my heart, and mind. These warnings were so real to me that it was as if I could hear the invisible angelic forces of God yelling at me to stop this Insane pursuit. Just retelling this event reminds me of another event that I experienced about five years later.

*Gods Audible Voice Said TO Me: YOU'RE A DEAD MAN! (1981)

At the time of this story, I was a pastor at three Springs Assembly of God. I was driving into Mount Union, Pennsylvania with my wife to do some grocery shopping. The vehicle that I was driving was a sports Ford Granada with a 302 Engine. The urge came to me to put the pedal to the metal and let it roar. The Lord had already delivered me from speeding years ago, but at that moment it was as if a devil took hold of me. I willingly gave in to this urge as I mashed down the gas pedal and began to increase my speed. Yes, I knew better, but I caved and gave into temptation. My wife looked over at me just shaking her head. (Someone else was watching our newborn son Michael, so he was not with us.)

I ended up accelerating to over 80 miles per hour. Kathleen was praying aloud that if we had an accident, she would not be hurt because of my stupidity, and then she began to pray faster in the spirit. I was coming around the corner on Route 747 right before you entered Mount Union when I heard the audible voice of God say to me, "You are a Dead Man!" Instantly the fear of the Lord hit me like a sledgehammer.

The fear of God went right to the very marrow of my bones. I saw a stop sign ahead of me to the left and to the right. At that very moment, I slammed on the brakes of my car, instantly slowing down. A flash of white zipped past my left. I mean right at once I saw a white, souped-up Dodge charger come speeding through the stop sign from the left.

He ran the stop sign without stopping or slowing up in the least. I mean he really had the pedal to the metal. I'm convinced he must've been going over 80 miles an hour. If I had not slammed on my brakes exactly when I heard the audible voice of God, his car would have slammed right into my driver's side door. There is no doubt in my mind or my heart that I would have been instantly killed. Thank God for his long-suffering and mercy.

<u>Back to my Insane Bike Riding</u>

Something evil and obsessive had gripped my mind and my emotions. Even though I knew that I was going to crash my bike and get myself killed, I could not seem to stop myself. These voices that were urging me on to go faster and faster were not only telling me to keep up with these men but were telling me that I should pass them at the first opportunity. Slowly but surely, they were leaving me behind.

Then as I entered a long stretch of road, I saw my opportunity to make my move. I began to catch up to them as I saw these riders begin to enter between two cliffs, one on the left side and one on the right. They seemed to slow down considerably right before they exited from these cliffs. It was time for me to make my move. I shifted my bike into high gear, opened my throttle all the way. My 750 took off like a speeding bullet.

Now I was coming up to them very rapidly when before I knew what happened, they completely disappeared from my sight. Inside of me, all kinds of alarm bells were going off. Voices were in my heart screaming almost in a panicking audible voice. Over and over these voices were telling me to stop this very minute. **They were telling me Not Just too slow down, but to Stop**! At the same time, other almost sinister voices were screaming to me don't stop, but speed up. You are about to catch up to them.

At that very moment, right before I had reached the end of these two high cliffs, I decided in my heart that I had had enough. It is like all the wind was taken right out of me. My stomach was all twisted, and my heart was hurting. Without giving it a second thought, I completely let up on the throttle of my bike. At the same time, I began to squeeze hard upon my breaks.

The bike responded immediately as I came to the end of these cliffs. The moment I came out from these cliffs it became obvious to me why the other motorcyclist had slowed up so drastically and then disappeared. The road in front of me disappeared into a 90-degree hairpin curve to the left. As I took the curve even at my slow speed, I was barely able, ever so scarcely to lean into it. Now, that was very frightening by itself alone. But what was really terrifying and heart wrenching frightening is what I saw just to the right of the road.

For there was nothing but empty air just three feet over the edge of the road. There were no railings on this curve, just gravel, and stones before a terrifying cliff. One of the highest cliffs that I had ever seen on my journey so far was right in front of me. It must have fallen away to the valley thousands of feet below, with a large rushing river at the bottom.

The sight of how high up I was into the mountains and the cliff that was before me took away my breath. If I had taken the curve just five miles faster, I would have never been able to make it. I knew in my heart that I would have gone right over the edge of the cliff, down to the river far below, never to be seen again this side of eternity. The road that I was on continue to run alongside this cliff on the left. It was some time before I could finally find a small resting spot where I could stop my bike.

I brought my motorcycle to a complete stop, and I slowly crawled off of my bike. My legs were shaking like Jell-O. My breathing was very heavy and yet shallow. I felt like I was going to pass out at any moment. I put my bike over on its kickstand.

I fell to my knees right there in the gravel, not caring if anybody saw me. I lifted my hands towards heaven, repenting for letting the demonic powers influence me to be so stupid. Crying out for God's forgiveness and help in the midst of my stupidity. And yet at the same time, I was overcome with the reality of God's long-suffering and Mercy.

CHAPTER FIVE

Logging Truck Trying to Kill Me!

If you have ever read my books, with all my experiences, you might wonder if these stories are true. My answer to that question is: **ABSOLUTELY YES!** My stories are not fabricated or exaggerated in the least. The craziest stuff has happened to me. This story I'm about to tell you really happened. This is really some strange stuff. This story reminds me of a TV movie that Steven Spielberg had made in 1971 called: DUEL!

It stars Dennis Weaver as a terrified motorist stalked on a remote and lonely road by the mostly unseen driver of a mysterious tanker truck. David Mann is a middle-aged salesman driving on a business trip. He encounters a rusty, old tanker truck on a two-lane highway in the California desert, traveling slower than the speed limit and expelling sooty diesel exhaust. Mann passes the truck, but the truck then roars past him and slows down again.

Throughout the film, this truck and its driver pursue David in his car. It was very strange in that the driver of this big Rig was out to kill David Mann for no apparent reason. The driver of the truck remains anonymous and unseen, with the exception of two separate shots where his arm waves Weaver on into oncoming traffic, and another shot where Weaver observes the driver's snakeskin boots. His motives for targeting Weaver's character are never revealed. Spielberg says that the effect of not seeing the driver makes the real villain of the film the truck itself, rather than the driver.

Amazingly I experienced something very similar. I had come to the beautiful mountains of Oregon. Now, this occurred in the summer of 1977, when I was 21 years old. As I drove my bike into the mountains of Oregon, I was amazed at the size of the trees that I saw. The trees that we had in Wisconsin were like toothpicks in comparison. My plan at this time was to go and see a good friend of mine and his wife, Lloyd and Bonnie Olds.

I was traveling at a very easy and comfortable pace. I had had enough excitement within the last week to last me a lifetime. My heart was still racing from my last experience of trying to keep up with those motorcyclists on ninjas. The fact that I was just seconds away from plunging over a thousand-foot cliff had truly shaken me up. It's amazing how fragile and fleeting life really is

I did not want to open the door for the devil in any way, shape, or form. I had become extremely careful in my driving realizing that there was numerous large wildlife throughout all of this area. The part of the journey that I had enjoyed the most was when I had driven through Yellowstone National Park. But still being on a motorcycle I had to be very careful around the buffalo, bears, and other large wildlife.

As I made my way through the back mountainous roads of

Oregon, I had passed up numerous logging trucks. The logs that they carried were overwhelming compared to the ones I had been used to seeing out East. With as many logging trucks as I was seeing, it was easy to assume that the logging industry must be one of the main sources of employment in this area. These large 18-wheel trucks with their humongous loads of trees really made me feel quite uneasy. The thought came to me that I would really hate to be in front of one of these trucks if it lost its brakes coming down a mountain.

At one point in my journey, I was going up a very steep incline of a very heavily wooded mountain. I noticed that there was a logging truck right in front of me with a full load of logs. The road was a little bit too curvy to pass the truck right at this moment. So, I decided just to wait patiently for the right opportunity. Right before I got to the top of this mountain, I could see that the way was clear for me to pass the truck. I began to pull around this logging truck, shifting my gears as I went. At the same time giving my 750 Honda motorcycle more throttle.

When I finally reached the halfway mark of passing the truck, something very strange, and dangerous happened. The truck driver began to pull his truck over into my Lane. The truck was virtually beginning to squeeze me right off the road. Whatever I was going to do, I was going to have to do it in a hurry. I was either going to have to give my bike full throttle, or slam on my brakes and get behind his truck again. I quickly decided to leave this logging truck behind with its unpredictable driver. I cranked the throttle of my bike even more. My bike took off like a rocket.

Just as I was about to pass the front of the truck, the front end of this logging truck literally came right over into my pathway. Without any doubt, I knew that I was a dead man if God did not supernaturally deliver me at this very moment. In order, not to get run over I had to take my bike into the loose gravel and Stones. Instead of slowing up I gave my motorcycle even more gas. My back wheel began fishtailing all over the place. I barely pushed past this large 18-wheeler, with its insane driver. The front bumper of the truck nearly brushed the right back crash bar of my motorcycle.

As I went past the truck driver, I did not slow down for one moment. I was determined to leave this logging truck and its driver as far behind as I could. It was not very long before I had gone over the top of the mountain, and had lost complete sight of the eighteen-wheeler which was behind me. The road that I was on was descending the mountain at a steep angle. Now on this road there did not seem to be very many curves. The ones that I did encounter were not very sharp, or dangerous.

Just when my heart was beginning to slow down, and I once again began to enjoy my ride, I felt a very strange sensation come all over me. It was like as if alarm bells were going off everywhere on the inside. I took a very quick glance in my rearview mirror, and to my utter shock, I noticed the same logging truck (with a full load of logs mind you) barreling down on top of my bike. I was so surprised by this truck sudden appearance that I cranked my head around to make sure that I was not seen things.

Sure, enough there it was, coming at me like an out of control train coming down the railroad tracks down a mountainside in a hurry. I knew in my heart at that moment that whoever was driving that truck was for some reason out to kill me. This man must've lost his mind, or was being driven by demons. There were tons of logs on that truck, so why this driver would be driving in such a reckless fashion? Immediately I began to shift my bike into higher gears, and at the same time, I cranked on the throttle. Once again, my bike took off like a rocket. Surely, I thought to myself that it would be easy to leave behind a fully loaded logging truck on a winding mountain road.

It probably would have been quite easy under normal circumstances, but not in this situation. This road I was on did not seem to have any sharp curves. Now, no matter what I did I could not pull ahead of this truck. It was catching up with me. Before I knew what was happening, the bumper of this logging truck was right up against my back tire. Fear filled my heart as I began to imagine what it would be like to be crushed underneath the chassis of this logging truck loaded with logs. It probably would feel a little like a mouse that was being stepped on by an elephant.

At any moment that truck was going to ram my back tire. I kept cranking my head around, to look at him. I could not see the driver through his windshield. This seemed to go on forever. At any moment, I was going to be chewed up underneath the engine, the frame, and the axles of this truck.

This was completely crazy and bizarre. Actually, it was demonic. This truck was breathing down my back neck, and there was no place I could see to get out of his way. I knew in my heart that if I made the slightest mistake, or if I slowed down just a little more, or if I took a curve wrong, that the truck behind me would flatten me like a pancake. It seemed to me like a never-ending nightmare right out of the twilight zone. No matter what I did, I could not get away from this crazy truck and its insane driver.

During all of this insanity, I did the only thing that I could think of doing. I began to cry out and ask God for divine deliverance. I knew in my heart that only God could deliver me from the madman in this logging truck. As I continued to pray and cry out to God, I noticed that the road began to become curvier right in front of me. I raced towards these curves as fast as I could, knowing that it was going to be my only chance to get away from this madman.

I came to these curves going faster than what I should, but just the other day I was able to survive curves that were much more dangerous. I leaned into these curves as my bike barely clung to the road. The good news is that it was working. The large loaded logging truck behind me had no choice but to slow up. I took advantage of this situation and continued to speed down the road much faster than what I should have. After I had left his large truck way behind, I was able to back off on my throttle.

A sweet aroma of peace began to envelop me as I continued to drive down the mountain road. When I finally arrived at the bottom of the mountain, I breathed a heavy sigh of relief. It was not long before I discovered the turn that I was looking for. This road would take me in the direction I needed to go. Thank God I never saw that logging truck again.

Amazingly during this whole experience, I never once felt any hatred, or bitterness towards the driver or his truck. I simply believed God to save my life. This is what the new birth had done for me. The divine nature of Jesus put me in a place of gratefulness instead of anger and hate. I have no idea what was going through that man's mind who was driving that big logging rig. But it was okay because God was with me and I know that it had been God that had saved my life once again.

Stabbed in the Face with a knife Multiple Times by a demon possessed women!

After I had arrived in Anchorage, it was quickened in my heart to stop at a small full gospel church that I used to visit. The Neighborhood Full Gospel Church. Now, It just so happened that an evangelist I had known while I was in the Navy on Adak, Alaska, was there. We spent some time reminiscing what had happened while we were in Adak.

He shared how the Lord had laid upon his heart to go to Pennsylvania to open up an evangelistic outreach center in a town called Mount Union, Pennsylvania. He invited me to go to Pennsylvania with him and his wife to open this evangelistic outreach.

I perceived in my heart I needed to go with them. I planned to fly back to Wisconsin where he and his wife would pick me up as they went through. However, before I left Alaska the spirit of God had one more assignment for me: a precious demon possessed woman needed to be set free.

One Sunday we decided to attend a small church along the road to Fairbanks. I was the first to enter this little, old, rustic church. When I went through the sanctuary doors, I immediately noticed a strange, little, elderly, lady across from me - sitting in the pews.

She turned her head and stared right at me with the strangest look I have ever seen. I could sense immediately there was something demonic about her. Out of the blue, this little old lady jumped up, got out of the pew, and ran out of the church. At that moment I perceived that God wanted me to go and cast the devils out of her.

When the service was over, I asked the pastor who that elderly lady was. He said she was not a member of his church, but she came once in a great while. He also told me that she lived with her husband in a run-down house on a dirt road. I asked him if it would be okay to go and see her? **(I knew in my heart that God had sent me there to help bring deliverance)** He said he had no problems with this, especially since she wasn't a part of his church.

We followed the directions the pastor gave us, and when we arrived at the house it was exactly as the pastor had described it to us. It was run-down, and the yard was overflowing with old furniture and household items. It reminded me of the TV show "Sanford and Son" - but it probably had ten-times more junk in the yard! I do not know how the old couple survived the winters in Alaska in such a poorly-built house. As we got out of the car, a little old man met us outside. It was her husband. He was thanking God as he walked toward us, and said he knew we were men of God, and that we had been sent by the Lord to help his poor, tormented wife. He informed us that his wife was in their kitchen.

So, we walked up to the house, having to go down the twisting and cluttered junk-filled path. We entered the house through a screen door that led into their summer kitchen. When we entered the kitchen, we could see his wife over at a large utility sink. Her back was to us, but we could see she was peeling carrots over her kitchen sink … with a very large, scary-looking, butchers knife!

As I stood there, looking at the back of her head, I began to speak to her about Jesus. Out of the blue, she turned her head like it was on a swivel to look at me. I could hardly believe my eyes! It was like I was watching a horror movie! This little lady's eyes were glowing red on her swiveled head.

I rubbed my eyes at that moment; thinking that maybe I imagined this. No … her head had swiveled - without her body moving - and her eyes were glowing red. Fear immediately filled my heart as she looked at me with the big knife … a butcher's knife … in her hand. Immediately, I came against the spirit of fear in my heart by quoting the holy Scriptures: **"For God hath not given me the spirit of fear; but of power, and of love, and of a sound mind"** *2 Timothy 1:7*. I shared with her about Jesus Christ.

The next thing I knew she was coming right at me - with her knife - as if she was filled with great rage. The knife was still in her right hand when she spun around and came at me. She leapt through the air onto me, wrapping her small skinny legs around my waist. How in the world she was able to do this - I do not know?! The next thing I knew, she was lifting up her right hand and hitting me in the face, very hard, multiple times. I could feel the pressure of her hitting me on the left side of my face. As she was hitting me in the face, out of my mouth came: "In the **Name of Jesus!"**

The minute I came against this attack **"In The Name of Jesus"** she was ripped off of me; picked up by an invisible power, and flung across the room about 10-feet or more. She slammed very hard against the bare wall of her kitchen, and slipped down to the floor. Amazingly when she hit the wall, she was not hurt! I went over to her, continuing to cast the demons out of her In the Name of Jesus. Once I perceived that she was free, and in her right mind, I asked her how she had become demon possessed? She told us her terrible story.

Her uncle had repeatedly molested and raped her when she was a very young girl. She thought she was free from him when he got sick and died. But then he began to visit her from the dead, continuing to molest and rape her at night.

To her, it was physical and real. She did not know it was a familiar spirit disguised as her uncle. This had probably gone on for over fifty years! I led her to the Lord. Sweet, beautiful peace came upon her, completely changing her countenance.

She was a brand-new person in Christ, finally free - after almost fifty years of torment. She and her husband began to go to church with us - until I left Alaska. I remember that we took them to see the Davis family at a local church, visiting Alaska on a missionary trip.

Years later, the evangelist who visited this lady with me, heard me retelling the story at a church; about how the woman kept punching me forcefully with her right hand. At the end of the service, he came and informed me that I was not telling the story correctly. I wondered if he thought I was exaggerating. He said that he was standing behind me when she jumped on top of me and began to hit me with her right fist.

But, he informed me, it wasn't her hand she was slapping me with … she still had the large butchers knife in her hand; and he saw her stabbing me in the face with this knife. Repeatedly!! He said he knew that I was a dead man, because nobody could survive being stabbed in the face repeatedly, with a large butcher knife.

He expected to see nothing but blood, but instead of seeing my blood everywhere, he saw that there was not even one mark on my face where the knife was hitting me. I did feel something hit my face repeatedly, but I thought it was her hand! Instead, it was her knife, and it could not pierce my skin! Thank God for His love, His mercy, and His Supernatural Divine Protection.

I am convinced that if I had not been walking with God in His holiness and obedience, the devil in that little old lady would have stabbed me to death. Many people in the body of Christ are trying to deal with demonic powers when they are out of the father's will.

When we are moving in the Holy Ghost, obedience, and absolute love for Jesus Christ - there is no power in hell that can hurt us!

My God hath sent his angel, and hath shut the lion's mouths, that they have not hurt me: forasmuch as before him innocence was found in me; and also before thee, O king, have I done no hurt (Daniel 6:22).

*Most of My Childhood Friends Dead

As I look back over my life it becomes obvious that God protected me even in all of my stupidity. Over 90% of the young men that I used to run with, hunt with, drink and drug with are dead. Most of them died terrible deaths. One friend fell asleep as he was going home late at night. His car went up an embankment, and hit a big oak branch coming from the tree. It took the top of his car off. We had a close casket funeral for him.

Two brothers Garry and Scott were barhopping on the lake where they lived. They knew the lake well. But one night as they were driving across the lake in a snowstorm, they got lost. They ended up on a part of the lake where the ice never freezes very thick because of the flow of the water. Their truck went down through the ice. They found their two bodies on the bottom of the lake. These two brothers were not near as foolish as what I was, and yet they died terrible deaths.

Claire who had saved my life on numerous occasions, once when I was drowning in my own vomit, was found dead. From all indications what he saved me from, is what killed him. He literally aspirated in his own vomit.

Famous celebrities who died by choking on their own vomit include Jimi Hendrix, Bon Scott, Tommy Dorsey, Tammy Homolka, and several others. Some celebrities died from inhaling vomit, choking on vomit while sleeping from a drug overdose, while others died from inhaling vomit due to alcohol consumption or alcohol poisoning.

Angels Kept Scaffolding from Falling Down

An evangelist and I had opened up an outreach center in Mount Union, Pennsylvania. The building was on the main street of Mount Union, being a former movie theater and theatrical facility. It was in need of much repair, having been vacant for many years.

We began to refurbish it from the entrance all the way back to behind the stage curtains and screen. I think the seating capacity was close to 600; about 400 on the first floor and 200 and on the second floor balcony. There was a lot of work to be done in the main auditorium. The paint and plaster were falling off ceilings close to 40 feet high.

For us to make the repairs, we had borrowed some old scaffolding from someone who was willing to let us use it. This was back in 1978 so my recollections are not the clearest as to the height of this auditorium. It might've been higher than 40 feet. I know one thing, it was really high up and we must've had at least eight sections of scaffolding stacked on top of each other to reach to the ceiling.

And, we still had to use extension poles in order to paint. Believe me, we were not using a lot of wisdom because this stack of scaffolding was extremely wobbly and unsafe. When you were on top of it, reaching towards the ceiling of the auditorium was very frightening. You had to move very, very carefully because the whole thing would sway by two or three feet, if not more. Every time that I climbed up to do plaster work or painting, I would cry out to God for his divine protection.

One day, as I was up on this scaffolding, a very notorious, wild and excitable Pentecostal brother came in. His name was Elwood and he was a Holy Ghost-filled brother known for his wild antics. He had a car with a PA system installed with speakers on the roof in order to go around preaching. We would do what I call a hit and run evangelistic outreach in the surrounding communities.

What do I mean by a hit-and-run? Usually we did this in the evening so that we would not be caught. He would stick the speakers up on top of the roof of his car; we would drive through a local community, turning the speakers up loud and preaching Jesus. Before the police would show up, we would split to another community. I'm not saying that this was using wisdom or was of God, I am simply stating that this is what we did.

So, Brother Elwood came into the auditorium shouting, "Praise the Lord, Brother Mike!" I was up on the very top already trembling and moving around very carefully. The minute he came in, I knew that I was in trouble. I was not wrong. I felt him grab hold of the bottom rungs of the scaffolding and begin to climb. I yelled down at him, trying to tell him not to come up because it was not safe even for just one man. He did not hear me because he was shouting praises to the Lord, getting all worked up and excited.

He kept on climbing as if this scaffolding was as solid as the mountainside. To this day I do not know why he did not recognize how it was all swaying back and forth as if it would fall over at any moment. My heart began to be filled with fear because I knew that we were about to come tumbling down. He finally got to the top, climbing in underneath the bars to where I was at. He was so excited that he began to pray and shout, crying out to God for souls; walking about on the top of this platform. This man truly loved praying, preaching, shouting and winning souls more than anything else!

I realized that there was no way that I was going to get Elwood to stop because he was going to pray, shout, dance, and whatever else as it came upon him. He was going to do what Elwood was going to do! I thought to myself, well if I'm going to die (I really believed this) I might as well die shouting with Elwood to the glory of God. So, I closed my eyes and joined in. We were praying, shouting, singing, shaking and moving about that scaffolding as if it was as solid as the Empire State building.

I guess that we must've been making quite a commotion because the brother that I had come with from Alaska came into the auditorium to see what all the commotion was about. He told me later that he could hardly believe what he saw because the scaffolding was swaying so bad that he knew it was going to come down at any moment.

He said that it was literally swaying back and forth, looking like it was about to tumble down at any moment. Actually, as far as it was leaning, there's no way in the natural that it could have continued to stand upright. He did not know what to do so he just stayed down below crying out to God for our protection. We must've prayed for at least 45 minutes, if not longer. I know this sounds incredible but I completely got lost in the Holy Ghost with brother Elwood.

The presence of God came upon us in a mighty way and we were having a Pentecostal, Holy Ghost, shaking and shouting service on the top of that old rickety, unstable scaffolding. I am positive that the angels of the Lord were standing all around us, keeping the scaffolding from tumbling down. Eventually we ran out of steam, sat down and just soaked in the presence of the Lord. God is so wonderful and merciful that even in our foolishness, He is there to help us!

Psalm 91:10 There shall no evil befall thee, neither shall any plague come nigh thy dwelling.11 For he shall give his angels charge over thee, to keep thee in all thy ways.12 They shall bear thee up in their hands, lest thou dash thy foot against a stone.

Life & Death based on the Report You Believe

Let me share a story with you that I was told is a true story. There were two men laying in the hospital in the same room. Somehow one of the nurses or doctors put the wrong chart at the end of the beds. A doctor came into this hospital room, while standing at the end of each bed he picked up the charts and began to read them.

The man who had a terminal disease was told by this doctor that his condition was minor. The doctor of course was reading the wrong chart at the end of this bed which had been switched with the other patient. The story goes on to say that this man with a terminal disease was filled with great joy when he was given the good news. Based upon the wrong chart, he was sent home, and lived for many years.

Now, the man who had a minor problem, was told by this doctor of his impending death. That he had a very serious illness and that they could not do anything for him. This particular gentleman was sent home to die, and he did die shortly thereafter. This man's imagination, his mind and heart was filled with gloom and doom from the wrong and negative report from this doctor.

If this story is true, both men were drastically affected by the information that were fed to them by the doctor. How much more serious is it when it comes to the word of God. Almost all mental and emotional illnesses begin within the human mind. We must bring our imaginations, minds, and wills into subjection, and in to the authority of Jesus Christ.

The devil loves us to take a molehill and make it into a mountain, and then there are mountains that need to be dealt with as mountains, and we treat them like molehills. Our imaginations need to be filled, crammed, and packed with the truth of God's word. Our mind is like an incubator, whatever eggs you plant within it, will hatch.

Our minds to some extent are like our bellies, which crave to be filled with food. Our belly really doesn't have much choice in what we are going to put in it. That is a matter of our own choosing. This is the same way when it comes to that which fills our imaginations. We can fill our mind with the images of that which God's word promises and declares, or we can put in them that which is against his will. There are well over 7000 promises in the Bible, and God wants to fulfill every one of these promises in our lives.

2 Corinthians 1:20 For all the promises of God in him are yea, and in him Amen, unto the glory of God by us

Overcoming Depression by the Word

Before I was born again, I was manic depressant, and suicidal. After I gave my heart to Jesus, February 19 1975, I was delivered.

Now here it was the winter of 1978, and depression was hitting me massively. I was living in that old chicken house with the evangelist and his wife.

I had moved all the way down the hallway to the farthest bedroom. I was sleeping on a plywood bedframe in my sleeping bag, in a room with no heat. My truck that I had just bought was sunk in a septic system, with a transmission that had gone out. I was having to walk almost 3 miles away to Belleville to go to work.

Wave after wave of depression was hitting me. I did not have enough money to fix my truck. There really was no food in the house. I allowed this to go on probably for better than a month.

One morning I got up to study and pray. That morning something snapped within my heart and mind. Enough was enough. I put my Bible on the floor, and stood on my Bible in my stocking feet.

I boldly declared: in the name of Jesus you lying spirit of depression, go from me, now! I am not going to put up with it one more moment, because Jesus has set me free. The minute I spoke the word of God against this depression, it released me. From that day forward I was free. Whom the Son Sets Free, Is Free Indeed.

God Delivered Me from a Girl Who Pursued Me 1977

As I was living in Belleville, Pennsylvania seeking God, something happened that I'm not proud of. I lived with an evangelist and his wife who I had joined up with to help start an outreach in Mount Union, Pennsylvania. During this time a young, born-again, spirit-filled lady who was quite pretty and about my age would come over to talk to this couple.

Whenever she would come over, I would walk outside and go up into the backfield where there was a large rock. There I would pray. I did this for two reasons: number one because I wanted them to have their privacy and number two because I wanted to pray.

This went on for many months, never really speaking much to this young woman. One day when she came over, she asked me what I was doing every time I left. I informed her that I would go and pray. She asked me if she could join me sometime; not thinking much about it, I agreed.

That was a big, big mistake. Before I knew what was going on, I began to become more involved with her. Next thing you know I was taking her on dates. I began to find my mind was thinking about her increasingly and not on the Lord. One night, after I had taken her out, she invited me into her house. I really did not think much about it because her parents were home. What could possibly happen with her parents at home? Her parents were in bed by that time.

We went into her front room where there was a couch. We sat down for a couple of minutes talking about different things when, unexpected, she asked me if I would massage her legs. Right then and there the *red lights* began to go off, but I did not listen to the Spirit of God. As she lay down on the couch, I began to massage her legs then her back —flesh against flesh. I do not need to go into any other details because you can already tell where this was going. No, we never did (thank God) go all the way or even close to all the way, but it was taking me down a path that I had no business being on.

Here I was, trying to go after God and now this new test had come upon me which I began to fail. Yes, this young lady had some problems, but I am not blaming her. I should have had enough God inside of me to say, "No, I'm sorry but I can't do that." I should've left! Instead, I opened a Pandora's Box in my mind, attitude, and heart.

Why do we just keep going around the same stupid mountains? Here's the answer: We always will until we learn that we must live by every word that comes out of the mouth of God! We are doomed to fall into the same ditches repeatedly until the Word of God becomes more real and important to us than anything that our mind mind, emotions or five senses may tell us.

Angelic Deliverance from seducing demons

Now I knew beyond doubt that I was in trouble. I came home one night all hot and bothered from being with her again and went to bed tormented. What I am about to share with you truly happened to me in a dream.

Almost immediately I fell into a restless sleep. As I slept, I found myself in a very realistic dream. In this dream I was entering a very large, plush bedroom. In the center of this room was a massive bed with silk covers and a brass frame. Lying on the plush, fluffy covers of this bed was two of the most beautiful and desirable women that I had ever seen; stripped to the skin. One of these ladies had long, flowing blonde hair with deep, hypnotic-blue eyes that seemed to swallow me up.

She reminded me of a tigress. The other one had coal-black hair that hung down to her chest. Her eyes were also coal black. She was like a wild black panther. The women seemed to be immediately aware of my presence and began to call and to beckon me, reaching their arms out toward me.

Immediately, I felt a very real and invisible power take hold of me. It literally began to drag me towards the bed. I began to fight it the best I could. In this dream, I literally leaned backwards against this power until my feet were in front of my body and my back was leaning up against this invisible demonic force.

With everything in my physical being, I kept struggling to stay away from this bed. But it was all to no avail. Step by step I was being dragged toward these two seductive women upon the bed. As they looked at me they were licking their lips like two hungry predators about ready to fill their bellies with their kill. Inch by inch I was dragged across the bedroom floor. I literally could hear demons somewhere in the background laughing, mocking me as I was dragged towards the bed. It was as if they were celebrating and relishing in my defeat.

As I was dragged closer and closer, these ladies' eyes demanded all of my attention. As I looked into their eyes, a shiver of absolute horror flowed down my spine. Their eyes were filled with such an evil that I had never known before or thought possible. I knew that there was no love whatsoever in their desire for me.

It was nothing but absolute lust and not just for me, but for anyone else that was gullible enough to yield to their enticements. This I also knew in my heart that once they devoured me, it would destroy everything that was decent and godly in my life. They would wipe their mouth, as the bible says, and declare that they had done no wrong.

Now I was only about two feet from them. There was no escaping them. Both women reached out to take my hands and pull me to them. I knew at once that I was a goner, trapped, caught — devoured by my enemy. I knew in my heart that they would consume me with their lust. As they finally succeeded in grabbing my hands, a cry came flowing from the depths of my heart and out of my mouth in this dream. "Oh, Lord Jesus, help me!"

"Oh, Lord Jesus, help me!"

As my knees hit the side of the bed, it was too late. They began wrapping their arms and legs all around me like an octopus, dragging me screaming and kicking into the pits of hell. At that moment, their beautiful faces became what they truly were: demonic and evil, even though their bodies stayed the same. I could not get away; they had me, and I knew it.

In this dream, just as I gave up all hope, I was transported above the bedroom. In my dream, I was looking down upon the bed. I saw the two women (demons) with hands upon my body. As far as I could see, there was no avenue of deliverance. There weren't even any doors by which I could leave the room. As they began to wrap their arms around my body, I noticed some type of movement off to my left side.

As I looked over in that direction, two of the largest men that I had ever seen walked right through the wall of that bedroom. In height, they were over seven feet tall. They were glowing with an unearthly light. Both had on large, white tunics and around their waists were belts of transparent gold. They both walked with a confidence and boldness that was beyond description. As I watched this scene unfold, the hair on the back of my neck and arms stood on end.

They were headed straight for my body, which was in a struggle against the two seducing spirits; demons of lust. As the angels got to me, one on the left and one on the right, they reached in right past the demons and grabbed me by the arms and the shoulders. They picked me up as if I was as light as a feather. They pulled me away from the bed, ripping me out of the hands of the two women who tried to hold on to me; but they could not. These two angelic beings were so much greater than the two she-devils that it was as if these demons were nothing compared to the strength of these amazing angelic warriors.

During this whole time, I was looking down upon the entire scene. And then, like a bolt of lightning, it dawned on me who they were (up until this time I had not realized). Angels that God had sent to deliver me, yes me, from the snare, enticements, and destruction of these devils. The angels turned their backs upon the women as they picked me up.

I was suspended between them as they carried me to the wall of the bedroom. When they reached the wall, I found myself no longer looking down upon what was taking place but rather I found myself between the two angels looking at the wall. Then to my absolute and utter surprise, the angels stepped right through the wall, taking me with them.

At that moment I found myself sitting up in my own bed. Now, I'm talking about my own physical bed in this tangible world. My hands were lifted in the air, praising and worshiping God. The Spirit of God was all over me and his presence was so thick and heavy that I cannot even begin to explain it to you. I immediately rolled out of bed, fell to my knees, and began to pray with tears rolling down my face and joy exploding in my heart.

It did not matter that it was only three o'clock in the morning. At that very moment, Jesus set me free from this stupid spirit of lust that had taken my mind and heart captive. Praise God! About three months later, God brought my precious wife to be into my life. After that experience, I had made a very real and strong commitment that I would never again seek relationships with people but I would go after God.

Romans 8:31 What shall we then say to these things? If God be for us, who can be against us?.

CHAPTER SIX
Jumped into a Frozen Pond

In the early spring of 1978 we were visiting a local State Park. At the state park there was a small lake. There is still ice over most of this lake, but there was a small hole where the ice had melted. This small opening was right at the end of a boat peer. We were, discussing stupid things we've done through the years.

The evangelist I was with said I would not have enough guts to jump into the lake. I told him with what I've been through up in Alaska, that's nothing. This discussion went on for a while. Before I even thought about what I was doing, I ran down the peer and took a flying leap. Down into the cold icy water I went. The minute I hit that water I literally believe my heart stopped beating. No one would be that stupid if at the pearly gates the Apostle Peter asked me: how did you get here? I think I would've been too embarrassed to tell him.

I was able to make it back to the surface of the water, swimming my way back to the peer and pulling my wet cold carcass up out of the water. Stupid me, I didn't even have any towels to get dry. I did not have any extra clothes with me. Without thinking I did that which was stupid. I wish I could say this was the last stupid thing that I ever did, but as you continue to read my books you'll find out that there seems to be an endless well of stupidity inside of me.

Spoiled tuna casserole

I came home one night from work, and I was extremely hungry. The couple I was living with were the ones who were to supply my meals. I gave them money weekly to cover my living expenses. When I came home the evangelist and his wife were gone. I began to rummage to the house to find some food. To my dismay there is no food available.

I opened up the refrigerator and it was completely empty except for a bowl of tuna casserole. It must've been sitting in there for weeks. But I was so hungry that I decided if I fried it up it be okay. After I had re-cooked it, I sat down to eat it. I guess when I prayed I wasn't operating in faith.

About an hour after I ate this tuna casserole, it hit my gut. Oh did I get sick! Wow, I cannot describe to you what I went through for the rest of that night. I could not stop vomiting and at the same time I had terrible diarrhea. In the natural I felt like I was going to die at any moment. Most likely I would have if God had not intervened.

I had affected my whole system with that spoiled tuna casserole. I laid on the plywood floor holding my belly and commanding this poison to come out of my body in Jesus name. I declared I would live and not die. Thank God I made it through the night, and by the morning I was ready to go to work even though I was still feeling rough. What did I learn from this fiasco? Do not eat old tuna casserole no matter how hungry you are.

Food Poisoning from spoiled Fish

What you can't smell can't hurt you, right? Wrong! Eating some kinds of spoiled fish can cause dramatic symptoms.

If the tuna is spoiled, you cannot deal with the poisoning by cooking or freezing the fish. Bacteria act on compounds in the fish, releasing histamine. This accounts for the allergic-type symptoms and also explains why antihistamines help control the symptoms. The fish most often responsible include tuna, mahi-mahi, mackerel, marlin, bluefish, amberjack, and abalone, though many others have caused scombroid poisoning.

Symptoms of spoiled tuna poisoning begin quickly, within about 15 minutes to 2 hours. This poisoning causes nausea, vomiting, diarrhea, muscle weakness, joint aches, headache, dizziness, and low blood pressure. A characteristic symptom is "hot-cold reversal"; hot items feel cold and cold items feel hot. Symptoms may begin within 15 minutes to 24 hours after eating affected fish. Most people are better in a few days, but in some cases symptoms have lasted for months or even years.

The Amway Spirit

Is there a Spirit of Amway? NO! And yet so many times God's people are deceived by demonic spirits and circumstances that look favorable for them to make big money. I know one Spirit filled older couple who are very close to us, who told us they had been suckered into over nine multilevel marketing programs through the years.

They informed us that they had never made any money, not even one time through these multilevel marketing schemes. People are sincere and excited about the business that they are launching off into completely convinced that it is God who sent this opportunity to them.

They want you to be a part of this wonderful money making the opportunity to make money for the kingdom. They're completely convinced that this is God leading them and guiding them, not realizing it's simply the lust of their flesh. They want you to be a part of what they're involved in because first of all, they need your participation to build their team. Then they need you to build your team to get a residue of your sales, to make them successful.

Through the years many people have tried to get me involved in this kind of businesses. Thank God that 95% of the time they have not been able to sucker me in. In the spring of 1977 and evangelist friend and I walked into a music store in state college Pennsylvania. As we were talking to the owner of the store, there is a gentleman dressed in a three-piece suit who was in his early 30s who approached us.

He wanted to know everything about our wonderful ministry in Mount Union PA. We shared with him about the work we were doing at our outreach ministry to the street people, drug users, and low income community. He informed us that he would love to come and visit us with the next couple weeks. That he would like to even make some contributions to help us in our endeavors.

When we left the music store, I informed my coworker that there just wasn't something right with this man. I told him I perceive there is some kind of spirit that it was upon him, operating through him. As we were driving back to Mount Union PA, it's like a light came on inside of me.

I told my coworker that I knew what spirit was operating in this man. He asked me what it was. I told him, **he's an Amway man**. He asked me what? I said this man was involved in Amway, and that he was going to come to see us to try to convince us to become a part of this multilevel marketing company.

Approximately one week later this man showed up at our ministry. He was extremely enthused about us, and in what we were endeavoring to do. He then informed us that he had a wonderful opportunity for us to fund our ministry. All he wanted was just a couple minutes of our time. We went into the office, with him carrying his briefcase.

When he opened up his briefcase, he would not come out and tell us exactly what he was involved in. It was a hush-hush, very secret, very profitable business that he was going to invite us to be involved in. Sure enough: It Was Amway! He wanted us to be involved so bad, that he even paid for me to be a part of it. I informed him that I had no desire to do multilevel marketing. I could not convince him to leave us alone. Eventually, he disappeared over the horizon. Many people are more excited about making money with wonderful opportunities than they are about the gospel of Jesus Christ.

I wish I could say that I never got suckered into any of these schemes, but in 2005 though, I fell for one of these schemes, hook, line, and sinker. Not only did I fall for it, but I got my wife involved, my oldest son, members of our church, and other friends. Yes, like a dummy I was led like a sheep to the slaughter. And yes, we all lost our shirts.

Please do not misunderstand me, I'm not saying that people cannot make a living off of these different endeavors. It's basically that you have to pour your whole life into trying to make them work. My purpose in life is not to get caught up in making money, but trying to win souls for Christ, and to see the captive set free. I find most people that get wrapped up in these schemes, are not looking truly at seeing people saved, but potential new representatives. Without really wanting to, they see a dollar sign written on your face.'

Momma G Cursing Calories

Many times as believers, we can be sincere in our heart, but wrong in the head. What do I mean by this? There is much Presumption in the body of Christ, especially in the part of the body that has embraced the Holy Ghost and the supernatural. Sometimes we try to exercise authority in situations and circumstances that we do not have the right to.

I think it goes back to the lesson we learned when Jesus was being tempted by the devil in the wilderness. After 40 days, Jesus was hungry. The devil showed up and told him that if he was the son of God, that he should turn those rocks into bread. Now, we know that without a shadow of a doubt, God could easily turn those rocks into bread to feed Jesus. The question is not whether or not God could, but was it his will? Jesus never exercised authority, power unless he heard the Father tell him to do it.

John 5:19 Then answered Jesus and said unto them, Verily, verily, I say unto you, The Son can do nothing of himself, but what he seeth the Father do: for what things soever he doeth, these also doeth the Son likewise.

John 5:30 I can of mine own self do nothing: as I hear, I judge: and my judgment is just; because I seek not mine own will, but the will of the Father which hath sent me.

I realize people are being taught that they can walk up to anybody they see that is sick, and pray for them. I'm not saying that you can't, I'm saying is it God's will? Don't be so quick to answer this question! Let me give you an example: Jesus walked by the man at the gate beautiful for 3 1/2 years. Why did not Jesus jump in, pray for the man, and get healed?

Now, anyone who comes to you, yes unless you have a strong quickening, not to you can pray for their healings. The man at the gate beautiful had an appointed time to receive his healing. God was going to use Peter after the day of Pentecost to heal this man. That day as Peter perceived it was God's day for that man, 5000 men came into the kingdom. There have been times when the Lord told me not to pray for somebody to be healed, without me understanding. I just simply strive to hear what God is quickening to my heart. That's all we can ever really do.

So back to my story: I used to visit Momma G's pizza shop all the time in Huntington. Many times I would sit down with her, and her restaurant workers to eat pizza. And Momma G would pray the stranger's prayer I ever heard. She would curse the calories in the pizza. God has not called us to curse calories. If you want to lose weight, stop eating the food full of calories. Now, I'm not picking on Momma G, but she was extremely overweight.

I knew Momma G for many years, and she was extremely overweight. All the cursing of the calories that she did every day, never stopped her from gaining more weight. I'm not picking on her; I see this happening all the time. Our lack of understanding of God's will gets us into trouble. I see people do this financially and I'm sorry to say I have done it too.

Instead of being content such things as we have, we get ourselves into financial difficulties by claiming that we were believing God as we buy things that we don't need. It might even be the fact that we know that God is going to bless us in a particular area, but the timing is not correct. We get the cart before the horse. In my younger years, we used to call it having ants in the pants.

Yes Momma G did die much sooner than she should have. She was a very godly woman, but we can all miss it in areas of our life. I know I have. Jesus help us. Why did you not correct her? Because in my heart there was a big red light. I knew in my heart by the Spirit of God she would not receive the truth from me!

My Firewood Business 1979

I needed to make some extra money to help cover the bills. I had my four-wheel-drive pickup truck, and all I needed was a chainsaw. A friend of mine said he had an extra chainsaw, and he would be willing to let me use it. The only problem was that in this part of Oklahoma they did not have a lot of forest, with dead standing trees. I did eventually fine a large piece of land that they were excavating for a new community.

On this large plot of land I found a huge dead trees laying on the ground. The wood was so hard that it took me a whole Saturday just to get one load of firewood. I then took it to a fellow Rhema student who had a large house with a fireplace. I knew that he needed some firewood.

He gladly bought the load of firewood from me at what the going rate was in that area. It was my first and last load of firewood that are sold. First it had been extremely difficult to cut this wood with a chainsaw.

Then I discovered that the man who bought it for me spent hours and hours trying to split it. And then he said it would not burn except if he put it on the top of his existing Goodwood that he was burning. That was the beginning and the ending of my firewood business.

Spiritual flake at Rhema

You will always find people in every Christian organization that are way out there. Rhema was no exception to this. There was one particular young lady who radiated flakiness.

Kathy and I during our time at Rhema tried to keep our nose in our own business. Wherever God is at work, you know the devil will be working there also. Towards our end of Rhema, there began to be a lot of grumbling going on among the students. Kathy and I began to listen to a little bit of this grumbling when the Lord spoke to me very strongly. He told me in my inner man, to not get involved.

To simply do what the Lord had told us to do. Receive the education and the training that we were there for, and then go into the harvest field. The day that we graduated from Rhema, our vehicle was already packed and ready to go. We had already notified our landlord. As we walked off the campus that day, we got into our vehicle, headed into the harvest field, and have never looked back.

Back to my story

There was one particular girl at Rhema as I was mentioning who was way out there. She would talk to you in a funny way, and she also walked in a floating manner. It was like she was trying to float everywhere she was going. She spoke with a mystical voice. That whole year I just simply avoided her. But one spring day, right before we were going to graduate from Rhema, she was walking in front of my wife and I going towards one of the main buildings on the campus.

Without thinking I spoke up. I spoke with a little bit of a loud voice and said behind her back: why are you walking like that? That got her attention immediately with her spinning around to stare at me. I told her: walking in the spirit, or being spiritual has nothing to do with acting like you are floating on a cloud, or changing your voice. I can truly say I did not say this in an ugly or mean manner. I was simply stating a fact.

Immediately her whole countenance darkened with storm clouds and lightning. If she truly was in this spiritual person she was putting on to be, she most likely would've just smiled at me, and kept floating towards the building. Instead, she began to yell at me, accusing me of being carnally minded. What we are full of will eventually be made manifest from out of our mouth.

At that moment I just simply smiled at her, and my wife and I walked right past her. As I was entering the building, she was still yelling at me from where she had stopped. From that moment to the time we left Rhema I never confronted her or spoke to her again. I just simply gave it to God.

If a person tells you that they are spiritual, or they want you to think they are spiritual, but attack you with a fit of deep anger, self-righteousness, or accusative attitude, you know they are not walking in the spirit of God.

James 3: 10 Out of the same mouth proceedeth blessing and cursing. My brethren, these things ought not so to be. 11 Doth a fountain send forth at the same place sweet water and bitter? 12 Can the fig tree, my brethren, bear olive berries? either a vine, figs? so can no fountain both yield salt water and fresh.13 Who is a wise man and endued with knowledge among you? let him shew out of a good conversation his works with meekness of wisdom.

14 But if ye have bitter envying and strife in your hearts, glory not, and lie not against the truth. 15 This wisdom descendeth not from above, but is earthly, sensual, devilish. 16 For where envying and strife is, there is confusion and every evil work. 17 But the wisdom that is from above is first pure, then peaceable, gentle, and easy to be intreated, full of mercy and good fruits, without partiality, and without hypocrisy. 18 And the fruit of righteousness is sown in peace of them that make peace.

If people ever begin to attack you, accuse you, yell and scream at you who claim to be Christians, simply walk away. Begin to cry out to God for their souls, that God would help them.

My Wild Time with "DUB"
George Wayne Hagin the *Older brother of Kenneth E Hagin*

Now, never in a thousand years could I have guessed that I would end up working for Rhema. But that was only the beginning of the surprise, but I ended up working with dad Hagins older brother, George Wayne "Dub" Hagin.

Even as brother Hagan was renowned in the body of Christ, so his older brother Dub had been renowned in the criminal world. Not only did Dub Hagan commit crimes before he was born again, but he was known for his ability to drive vehicles for criminals as the getaway driver.

The getaway driver's official name is = Partner in crime, aka, P.I.C; and is probably the most essential person in a group of bandits. This person must be the "eyes" and needs to keep a look out for the authorities or anything/one who could be the demise of their plans. The P.I.C must keep a level head and stay calm so that the robbery can be completed effectively and skillfully to its completion. Not to mention, the P.I.C is the one who must deal with the aftermath of their deeds and has to be prepared for anything, because even though there is a plan, anything could happen. Ultimately, it's the P.I.C's duty to keep the gang out of jail.

Brother Hagin knew what his brother was doing, and struggled with the fact of his brother being able to get saved. Through the years Hagin has shared small portions of his older brother's shenanigans. He also gave us insight to the spiritual travail that he had gone through himself to see his brother Dub get saved. Before I share my experiences with Dub, let's take a look at what brother Hagin said about his brother.

<u>Brother Hagins Story!</u>

Intercession does not change God, God never changes. Prayer does not change God. Prayer changes you, and it changes others. It does not change God.

I saw what I had to do for my brother Dub by the spirit of God. I'd been fasting and praying that God would save him off and on for over 15 years, and if it ever did any good, I couldn't tell it. Now in our younger years my oldest brother, Dub, had to live with some kinfolks, and I lived with others. We both grew up with chips on our shoulders. Dub was the black sheep of the family. Anything you could mention, he'd done. If some of our kinfolks did Dub wrong, he'd whip them. During those years I couldn't start anything because I had a heart condition.

God gave me a revelation of the authority of the believer. I knew in my heart that if I could break the power of the devil over older brother Dub, that it would work for anyone.

I rose up off the bed with my Bible in one hand, and the other hand lifted toward seven, saying, "In the Name of the Lord Jesus Christ, I break the power of the devil over my brother Dub's life, and I claim his deliverance. (That meant I claimed his deliverance from that blindness, that bondage of Satan.) And I claim his full salvation in the Name of the Lord Jesus Christ."

Within three weeks, my brother was born again. Now a day came after his salvation that Dub had a terrible accident and was in the process recuperating. He came to my home in Texas and was very depressed because his wife had left him and taken the children while he was gone. While I was preaching in church on Sunday morning, I had a vision. I saw my brother in the city park. I heard Dub say that he would kill his wife and himself.

During this visitation brother, Hagin stopped his sermon and took spiritual authority over the situation. He said to the enemy, "Devil, you stop that right now! I command you in the name of Jesus to leave that man." Then he continued his sermon.

When brother Hagin got home, his brother had returned to his house and was in good spirits. He said he had walked to the park and had decided to take matters into his own hands. Rev. Hagin said he knew and shared with Dub about his vision. Dub said he felt a cloud lifted from him suddenly and he came back to the house whistling and singing. Brother Hagin shares in his testimony that even though his older brother had gotten born again, it took a lot of work and prayer to see him continue walking with God.

MY WILD EXPERIENCES WITH DUB HAGIN!

When I began to work for Rhema, Dub Hagin was still young in the Lord. He basically was a driver for the ministry. When they would go on Crusades or meetings Dub would drive one of the trucks that pulled a trailer full of equipment and supplies to the meeting. I can tell you one thing for sure he loved to drive a pickup truck that had been souped up. As we would drive down the highway, most times Dub would be speeding. I would ask him to please slow up, but he never seemed to hear a word I said. The more I asked him to slow up, the more he would speed up, looking at me with a large grin.

Stupid Is As Stupid Does

I remember sitting in the front bucket seat as he was shifting his gears, racing down the main Highway, or back country roads. The biggest smile you ever saw would come upon his face as he put the petal to the metal. The more I asked him to slow up, the faster he would go. My was he in his element as he drove that vehicle as fast as he could wherever we were going. Now, brother Norvell Hayes is known for having only two speeds: slow, and slower! I can tell you that Dub Hagin only had two speeds: Fast and Faster Yet!

Dub told me in detail how that when they had bought this particular pickup truck, he had the engine removed. Then he had that engine taken to an engine machine shop where they bore out the cylinders, changed the heads, and put special exhaust manifolds on it. He had special carburetors that were designed to go on a high-rise manifold. He told me everything was blueprinted and built to exact specs. I cannot remember what horsepower he told me it was. It has been over 39 years ago when I was with him.

All I could do as he was shifting gears, grinning, racing down the highway was to pray in tongues and in English. Like I said even though I yelled at him at times like as if he was just an old friend "Dub you need to slow up"! He would just smile even bigger, and try to get the truck to go faster.

I think this is where Kenneth Hagin Junior got his love for driving fast. When we were at Rhema, you would hear Junior on the back portion of the property racing down a straightaway that he had built. I would stand in the yard at Rhema working outside after-school, hearing him revving the engine of his race car, and ripping and tearing down a straightaway. Lol!

Now one-day Dub and I were together in the pickup truck loaded with house furnishings that we were taking to brothers Hagins new house. Now, this house wasn't exactly new, it was old and in a very distinguished community. Supposedly somebody had given him this very nice stone house, with a stone wall all the way around the backyard. It reminded me of an old English manner.

I never asked any questions about this house or other things that brother Hagin owned, because it was none of my business. I do remember standing in the house in a beautiful sunk in front room listening to brother Hagin talking to his older brother Dub trying to give him instructions. I had never personally ever spoke to Kenneth Hagin. I just simply thank God that I had the privilege to be around him.

<u>So back to my story</u>

So Dub and I were headed over to Kenneth Hagan's house with a load on the back of this souped-up, dully, pickup truck. We were on a 2 Lane Hwy. We were on the left-hand side when a red sports car pulled up to us. (I'm not attacking Dub-he just simply still had a lot of the old gangster in Him that needed to be gotten out). This red sports car pulled up even with us coming down the highway.

I saw the glint in Dub's eyes! I told him very bluntly: Don't Do It, Dub! He simply looked over at me and grinned. He put the pedal to the metal wanting to race this sports car. Well, sure enough, it was the red sports car versus Dub Hagins souped-up, blueprinted, and specially built, heavy duty dully, pickup truck. The person with the sports car gave it all they had to get ahead of us. But they could not get past Dub. Dub would actually get ahead of the sports car, and then would back off a little in order to be side-by-side with the other car.

Signs began to appear that the two-Lane Highway was going to be coming to an end. I could see the two-Lane Road was going to become one lane, so I very strongly encouraged Dub to back off, or to get ahead. I'm not exaggerating; he just grinned at me even more.

Now it began to get very precarious, the person we were racing could see that he was going to run out of Road Ruth soon. He would speed up, and Dub would speed up. The sports car would slightly slow down, and Dub would slow down. During this whole time, I'm yelling at Dub, commanding him to stop it. But he simply ignored me, acting like as if I wasn't even there.

Now I can really understand where Dub was coming from. You see I used to run with a gang out of Chicago. And when I was in the world we were always playing chicken with our vehicles, and racing cars. I would not like to tell you the things that we did because they were not of God.

I remember when I was 17 years old driving my Mustang through a swampy area of Racine Illinois. I saw a vehicle coming towards me on a long straight stretch, and so I went over to that vehicles side with my Mustang. We were headed right towards each other, and I refused to move.

I still remember to this day the fear that was in the eyes of the people in the other car as I was about to hit them head-on with my Mustang. Something in me (the devil) would not let me go to my side. The last I saw of that vehicle is that they had to veer off the road into the swamp.

Now here I was with brother Hagins older brother Dub, looking like we were about to experience a major accident. I'm yelling at the top of my lungs by this time: Dub stop, stop it right now. I looked down over at the person in the sports car, and so all that their eyes were as big as soup bowels or at least they seem to be that big to me.

Right when it seemed like it was all over for the sports car which was about to run off the road into trees, Dub put his foot to the brakes, letting that poor soul get in front of us. It definitely was a wake-up call for that person whoever it was to get right with God.

I am not making any of this up; I am simply stating the facts. The only one I ever told about this incident was my precious wife. When I went home to my wife, I never spoke evil about Dub because I knew that God was still working with him.

Now, Dub has been gone to be with the Lord for many years, and brother Hagin is gone, with so many of the precious saints who have had a wonderful influence upon my life. They have reached a level of perfection and maturity I can only imagine.

The day will come when I will be with them and Dub once again. I can imagine dub and me together in the chariot being pulled by Angelic Heavenly Horses. I can see myself standing beside him hanging on to the edge of the chariot with white trembling fingers as he is taking the chariot for a spin. I can imagine him looking over at me with the biggest grin you can imagine, having the time of his life!

Dealt with an Epileptic Seizure in a Church

My wife and I had completed Bible College, moving back to Pennsylvania to pastor a small church. Basically God had put it upon my heart to pay off the debt of this church (independent), and to close it down for that it would not leave a bad witness in the community. Once this was completed we began to attend different churches as the spirit of God let us. On one Sunday morning my wife and I attended an Assembly of God church in Three Springs, Pennsylvania. As the guest speaker was preaching there was a commotion about six pews in front of us.

Stupid Is As Stupid Does

A woman who was probably in her late 30s had gone into a terrible epileptic seizure. She had fallen off of her pew, and was now laying in the aisle between the pews kicking and flailing about. What was so strange is that everybody in the church ignored her, and the **speaker Kept Preaching** like everything was normal. My wife and I looked at each other wondering what in the world was going on. I asked the lady next to us in a whisper what was happening. She whispered back, informing us that this lady had seizures all the time, and there was nothing they could do. Everybody had simply learned just to act like nothing was wrong.

I could not believe what I was hearing. There was no way that I was going to sit here watching this woman tormented by the devil while this pastor continued to preach. I whispered to my wife, telling her I would be right back. I got up out of my pew, walking up to the pew where she was still having this seizure on the floor. I walked over to where she was having her seizure, and bending down to put my hands on her squirming body. I **whispered**: you Foul spirit in the name of **Jesus Christ loose her Right Now**!

Then I removed my hands waiting for the manifestation of my command to be fulfilled. Within less than one minute she stopped squirming, her eyes refocused, and she was okay. I helped her get up to sit down. Her mouth and her face was covered with spit and saliva. I could tell that this particular lady was not altogether there mentally. When I was done helping her, I went back to my pew.

During this whole time the congregation just went on with the service, and the speaker just kept preaching. Even though this woman desperately needed help, they had not helped her. **Why?** I believe it is because they did not understand the authority that we have in Jesus Christ, when we are submitted to God. Now this is not the end of this story.

Disappointed with Ministers Conference
1979

When I was embraced by the Assembly of God denomination as a minister of the gospel, I thought maybe I had found a place where I could really grow spiritually. I was still a young buck at the age of 23, and desperately wanting to grow spiritually. They invited me to a ministers gathering. I was so excited that I went out and bought myself a leisure suit. At the time I was basically a Levi and silk shirt man.

I sat down with men that were twice to three times my age. In my heart I thought they would teach me how to be more effective in my prayer life. Surely they would teach me how to be successful in winning souls. I was positive they would train me in how to disciple the people of the church I was pastoring. That this moment with these mature men of God would be a life-changing experience for the furtherance of the kingdom.

I'm sorry to say it was everything but what I thought it would be. Now, this was back in 1979. I have no idea what the emphasis among the ministers in this denomination are in this day and age. At the writing of this article it is 2019.

So what did they teach me? They began to teach us how we could get more money from the congregation. They were teaching us how we can have better retirement benefits. Also how to get the board to agree to a better healthcare plan and a bigger salary. I'm not sharing this story in order to slander the denomination or its ministers, I am simply sharing with you the facts of what I experienced. Eventually, I simply let my credentials run out, credentials which many men covet and desire.

I walked away from that gathering with a very heavy heart. In over 40 years of pastoring since that time, I have never felt any bitterness, resentment or anger towards those men. All I know is I had a heavy heart. I wanted to be spiritually challenged and edified as a young minister, instead I walked away with nothing but an empty feeling in my gut. Why are you writing this then? It is a part of my life history, my memoirs, what I have experienced as I have walked this road called life.

I did not, and will not allow disappointments to prevent me from pursuing the will of God. Those disappointments can come from denominations, other people, or even your own failures, but just get back up and keep on going for Jesus. This life will soon be passed, and only what you do for Christ will last.

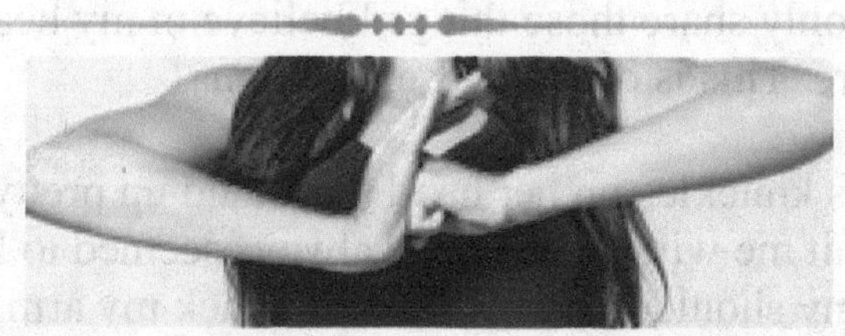

PUNCH for PUNCH!

My wife has always been a kind of tomboy. She's not one of these delicate easily hurt and offended women, thank God. Her upbringing was rather rough-and-tumble being oldest in the family with two brothers and a sister.

Her father died when she was only eight years old. Her stepfather was a violent twisted man. She had to learn how to defend herself. She's not one of these women that will lay down and play possum. Thank God she got born again at a very early age which helped her from becoming contaminated by what she experiencing.

Now, I had been raised in a home where my dad would hit my mother. One time he even broke my mom's jaw. I would have been exactly like my natural dad except I gave my heart to the

Lord on my 19th birthday. Within my heart of hearts, I said to myself: you will never hit your wife if God gives you one.

After my wife and I were married, there would be times when we had disagreements. I never raised my hand to my wife, though I did raise my voice. My wife would get so frustrated with me, that she would take her right fist, and hit me in my shoulder. It may not sound like a woman could hurt a man, but she would put the hurt on me.

 Yes, I'm sharing intimate and personal experiences in my life. That's one thing I like about the Bible, is that it does not try to cover up, sugarcoat, or hide anything that happened in the life of the saints. Now it does not give you every detail of every situation, in which I think we should be very grateful. In my memoirs, I only share those things I believe in my heart that I need to share. This is one of those situations.

My wife has knuckles on her hand that stand up pretty high. When she would hit me with her fist, she always seemed to know exactly how to hit my shoulder. The pain would rack my arm, and I would try to rub the pain out.

In the beginning, when she first began to hit me, it was far and in between. But from August 1978 until the spring of 1980 it was really getting bad. I begged her to stop hitting me, and by God's grace, I never hit her back. It was getting so bad that I went to the Lord in deep prayer. It was happening on a daily basis and even at times more than once a day.

When I went to the Lord in prayer, I asked Him what I should do? The Scripture that came to me is: Give and It Shall Be Given Unto You, Good Measure, and Pressed down. Surely this could not be God? But it was very strong in my heart, and not based on anger or bitterness.

I went to my lovely wife and told her what I felt the Lord said to me. I said: baby doll every time you hit me in the shoulder with your fist, I am going to hit you back just as hard if not harder. I said I want you to understand that I am not angry with you, or bitter. I do not want to hit you back, but it is getting worse every day with you hitting me. After I said this to her as I was looking into her eyes, I walked away.

It might've been the same day when she got angry at me about something. She hit me in my shoulder the way that she normally does. My, did it hurt or did it hurt? When I was a young man growing up I would trade punches with other men my age, but they never seem to hurt as bad as when my wife hit me with her bony knuckles. I looked her in the eyes and I said: I love you baby doll, and then I punched her in the shoulder. Oh, I could see that it really put the hurt on her. But instead of backing down, she hit me again even harder.

I told her ahead of time, I'm so sorry baby doll. And then I slammed her in the shoulder with my right fist. Once again she was really hurting. This Punch for punch kept going back and forth until finally, something broke within her.

I think she began to cry, and I took her in my arms and comforted her. I know it's hard to believe, and I know this sounds really cruel, but it broke this terrible habit that she had given herself over to. Maybe just a couple times in the last almost 40 years has she ever hit me in the shoulder again. Then we would have to go just for a little bit through the same process.

Please don't misunderstand me I am not in any way form or fashion advocating abuse torture made, I am simply sharing with you something that happened in our lives and in our marriage. I am not saying that this is the answer for you, but for some strange reason, it was for us.

CHAPTER SEVEN
Stop Saying You Can't Remember

One morning as I was in prayer, it seemed like as if Scriptures I had memorized had simply disappeared from my mind. I was so upset that I could not quote from Scriptures I said to my wife: Honey I think I'm beginning to forget Scriptures.

She did not respond. The next time I went to quote Scriptures, it was worse than the time before. I reemphasized to my wife that I was forgetting Scriptures.

This seemed to go on for a number of weeks, and before I knew what was happening, I was no longer being able to not just quote Scriptures, but memorize them.

One day as I was in prayer, I was complaining to the Lord. I said Lord: I'm losing my memory, and I can't remember Scriptures. Out of the blue I heard the Lord very strongly speak into my heart with almost an audible voice: **you are simply Getting What You're**

128

Saying.

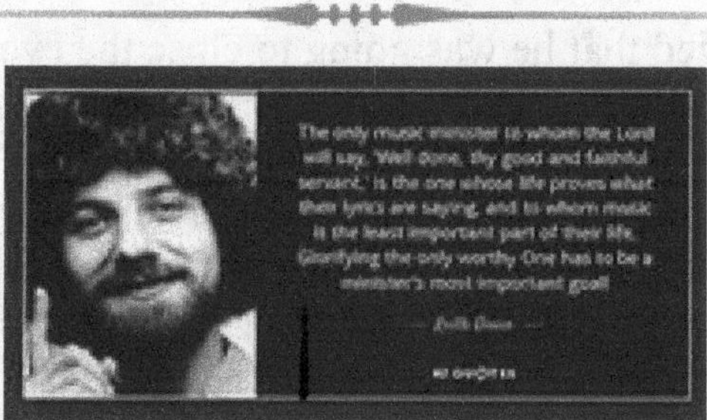

Stupidity Got Keith Green Killed

Now, Keith Green was one of my favorite Christian artist. We can be right in the heart, but wrong in the head. Because I was still connected To Agape Camp Farm, they would give me free tickets to the concerts. We would volunteer to help in whatever area we could. I discovered that Keith Green was going to be one of the singers at the 1980 Christian concert gathering. I could not wait to hear Brother Keith. His songs were so convicting.

I sat with the multitude of people with my wife waiting for Keith to come and sing and speak. Keith finally came, and the crowd erupted in cheers. In the beginning, we were really moved spiritually by his songs and his encouragement. But as time went on things shifted.

He began to preach a message that was extremely condemning. Please do not misunderstand me, I strongly believe in the Holy Ghost and conviction of sins. Only God can bring true conviction, but if WE TRY to force people to obey, repent, and serve God, it will have the opposite effect.

I know what I'm talking about because I was born again under a heavy wave of God's conviction, with the fear of the Lord. Keith, in my opinion, was trying to make us come to a place of total surrender. The whole atmosphere was completely changed. His time to be on the stage came and went. The next speaker, Barry

McGuire who was also one of my favorite singers and speakers never took to the stage.

Keith had decided that he was going to close the event that night. He refused to leave the stage when his time was over. This is not gossip, this is the truth. Because I knew the staff at Agape Camp farm they told me the whole terrible story. You see most of the staff at Agape at that time attended the church I was pastoring. As Keith was on the stage they were trying to figure out how they were going to get him off. They asked Barry McGuire what they should do. He simply said, just leave him alone. I'm okay, I'll live another day to sing and minister.

It is so sad when we get so full of ourselves that we think if we do not do what needs to be done, it will never get done. It could be that Keith repented after this incident, I do not know. I do know he died in a terrible plane accident just two years later.

Because I have been a pilot in the past, there are just certain things you cannot get away with. One of them is overloading the plane with too much weight. A friend of mine knew Keith personally and had told Keith numerous times that if he did not stop making his pilot overload the plane, they were going to end up in a terrible accident. I'm sad to say, it happened.

Death in a plane crash

Along with eleven others, Green died on July 28, 1982, when the Robertson STOL-modified Cessna 414 leased by Last Days Ministries crashed after takeoff from the private airstrip located on the LDM property.

The small two-engine plane was carrying eleven passengers and the pilot, Don Burmeister, for an aerial tour of the LDM property and the surrounding area. Green and two of his

children, three-year-old Josiah and two-year-old Bethany, were on board the plane, along with visiting church planters, John and Dede Smalley and their six children. Green's wife Melody was at home with one-year-old Rebekah and six weeks pregnant with their fourth child, Rachel, born in March 1983.

The National Transportation Safety Board (NTSB) determined that the crash was caused by the pilot in command (PIC) allowing the aircraft to be loaded beyond its operating limitations. The required pre-flight weight and balance computations responsibility of civilian pilots would have shown it was dangerously overloaded and also outside its weight and balance operating envelope.

PS: From a Response on Facebook!
By Charles Finney

Loved Keith Green dearly, and been listening to his music for almost 40 years. I hate it when Christians claim that God took him home, it's somehow part of his mysterious plan and sovereignty, that God is in control, and all the other nonsense they say. God had nothing to do with Keith's plane crash. Your story tells the truth.

 I remember that Melody, his wife said that as they said goodbye to each other before he got on the plane there was this strange feeling and awkward moment between them, almost as if they both knew they were saying goodbye to each other. That right there should have caused both of them or at least one of them to say this is a bad idea don't go!

Losing Keith Green was a tremendous blow to the body of christ, especially to the contemporary Christian music scene, which after his passing has become totally worldly, money driven, and corrupt. I haven't been able to listen to Christian radio for 20 years because the music is no different than the world's, and it is fleshly garbage.

Keith would have been a gatekeeper and his influence could have been used of the Lord to thwart the shameful folly of what contemporary so-called Christian music turned into. So the devil was able to exploit this and get rid of a man we truly needed.

* * *

1981

But What If Our Sons Marry Their Daughters

We had been bussing to our Sunday morning approximately 40 to 50 African-Americans from the projects in Mount Union Pennsylvania. About 30 of them were children. In 1981, these children seem to be very well behaved. All of these people were very hungry for God. We had seen him get born again and filled with the Holy Ghost. They were eager and enthusiastic worshipers of Jesus.

One day I was over at one of the major board members house. He had two sons that were 7 to 9 years old. Out of the blue he looked at me seriously and said: what are we going to do if our children want to marry these black kids? He really threw me for a lopper. I said what in the world are you talking about? He said: you know, our sons might want to marry their daughters.

I was really kind of dumbfounded for a moment. You see in my heart and mind I believed that in God's eyes there is no difference between any believers no matter their nationality, color of skin, ethnic background, or monetary position in life. In my heart and mind, we are all one in Jesus Christ. It wasn't too long after that, my wife and I left this church. Immediately, I mean right away (it must've been the board who decided) they stopped running the bus.

My concern for my sons and my daughters were never about

them getting married to someone of another color, race, or background. My only concern is that they married someone who was deeply in love with Jesus Christ.

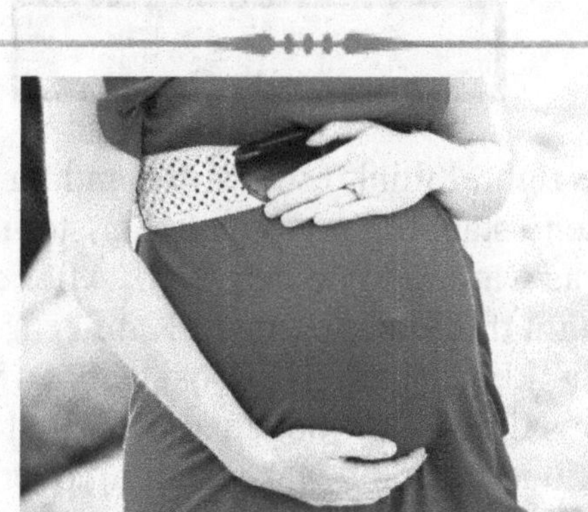

Kathee pregnant, a Girl a with knife
1981

Kathleen and I were having the youth gather in our parsonage. Many of these young people were from rough backgrounds. They were coming from all around the county. In this gathering, there was a girl who was about 18 years old. She was very rough and aggressive. It turns out that she was dating one of the boys in our youth group who was only 16 years old.

One night as we were gathered, this 18-year-old girl found out that her 16-year-old boyfriend was dating another girl in the youth group. She pulled out a large knife that she was going to use to stab this other girl who was seeing her boyfriend. Now, my wife was eight months pregnant with Michael, our first child. As she went after this other girl my wife stepped in between her and the one she was trying to stab. I can still see in my mind's eye that day. My wife standing there eight months pregnant, with her belly protruding in front of her. This girl was trying to get around my wife and was swinging the knife in stabbing very erratic ways.

Horror filled my eyes as it looked like at any moment she was going to end up stabbing my wife in the stomach. My wife was standing there with great authority, commanding her to stop. There is no fear in my wife's eyes whatsoever. I was operating in fear at that moment and was frozen in place. My wife was able to take the knife away from this girl and to end the fight.

Even after the fight, I think I was still standing petrified. That knife got so close to stabbing my wife in her stomach, where our newborn baby was waiting to be delivered. After everybody left that night, I brought this situation up to Kathleen. I said: baby doll, what were you thinking. That girl almost stabbed you in the stomach numerous times. She looked at me with total confidence and peace and said to me: God was watching over me! That was the end of the conversation.

Who Voted? (Living Word Assembly)

It got into my silly head that in order to get the church to grow even more we needed to change the name from: three Springs Assembly of God Church, to the new name: Living Word Assembly!

I went to the board to try to convince them. They seemed reluctant, but I convinced them to put it before the congregation as a vote. I stood before the church for a number of Sundays encouraging them that we needed to have a name that was more exciting and visionary.

Now, my wife and I were not members, but we were the pastors, so we were not allowed to vote. On a Sunday the official vote was to happen, I told my wife before the service, baby doll you need to vote! She told me, honey I'm not supposed to vote. I basically said, you need to vote. She said okay, I will because you're telling me to, but I'm not supposed to.

Well, the vote took place, and the board counted to vote. It came back unanimously that the new name of the church was going to be Living Word Assembly.

Well of course I was happy. Then they brought up the strange fact that they had one more vote than what they had members. Now, it had completely slipped my mind that my wife had voted. I believe it was God trying to teach me a lesson. I said to them, I wonder who voted? Now, I was very sincere. We began to ask around, who voted who's not a member? Now, remember it had been taken from my mind that I had told my wife to vote even though she wasn't a member.

Suddenly, my wife spoke up. She said I voted! The mainboard leader said: why did you vote? You weren't supposed to vote, you're not a member, and you're the pastor's wife. She answered and said: yes, I know that. The board member asked again: why did you vote then. I'm standing there completely in the dark. I'm not even thinking the thought that I had told her to vote.

The second time he asked my wife said: My Husband Told Me to! He told me even though I was not to vote, that I should vote. I stood there with egg on my face, and I could not deny it. The board, and the congregation just looked at me. I just kept my mouth shut.

Well Known Preacher Will Fall to Prostitutes

One of the members of the church gave me a book to read from a well-known evangelist. This particular book was on the subject of faith. I was very interested in reading it because I wanted to see what he had to say on this subject as this was an area in my life where God had placed upon me a great demand. Over and over in the last seven years I had to move in faith in order to be healed, delivered, protected, set free, and for our needs to be met. As I was reading this book my heart was filled with sorrow. Some personal tragedies had taken place in this man's life and in the lives of those he had loved.

He had not seen his prayers answered the way he thought they should be. Based upon these experiences, he had been teaching a doctrine of faith which did not line up with the Bible. In the process of embracing his own self-made doctrine, built upon his experiences, he was cutting himself off from all that God had made available for him. Not only was he cutting himself off from wonderful experiences, but he was leading all of those who followed him into the same misguided and wrong philosophy.

I'm sharing this with you not to be critical of anyone, but Scripture says that if any man thinks he stands, let him take heed lest he falls. I'm sharing this to help people come into the place where they can experience a continual flow of the Holy Ghost and the miraculous. As I continued to read that book, the Spirit of the Lord spoke to my heart and said, that if this man ever fell, (not that he would fall into sin) it would be to prostitutes.

It is actually frightening when God begins to tell you specific things, especially when it comes to judgment or repercussions of disobedience. I told my wife what the Spirit of the Lord Had spoken to my heart. I am sorry to say that a number of years later it was revealed that he had fallen to prostitutes. Now what in the world would this have to do with this book? We need to connect the dots. What is the victory that overcomes the world? Read Hebrews chapter 11. Look at all of these great woman and men of God. How did they overcome? By faith! But faith in what, or whom? (Lord willing that's another book.)

For whatsoever is born of God overcometh the world: and this is the victory that overcometh the world, even our faith. Who is he that overcometh the world, but he that believeth that Jesus is the Son of God? (1 John 5:4-5).

Doctor Who Would Not Listen

The Dr. that we were using for the birth of Michael, was the original Dr. who had overseen the birth of my wife, plus her mother. Now, my wife and I had done research about childbirth. There's a procedure they call episiotomy in which right before the babies given birth to, the doctor makes an incision. Between the vaginal opening and the anus. In our research it seemed to us that this was not always necessary.

Kathleen and I had prayed about whether or not this procedure should be used on my wife. We both felt in my heart it was not necessary. When we had our meeting with the doctor before the birth of Michael we told him without any ifs, ands or buts, that we did not want this procedure. He seemed to argue with us some telling us that in all of his years that he had never seen a situation where women did not need it. We told him, we did not want it. He simply stared at us.

It turns out that in those days it was just naturally practiced, no matter what. And yet doctors are supposed to fulfill the wishes of their patients. Well, when my wife went to go give birth, and our baby was right there, ready to come forth. This Dr. completely ignored our wishes. As a result of this incision, it took some time for my wife to heal up. It actually turns out that a straight cut instead of a minor tear, is much harder to heal if in most cases they would've let nature take its course. There is, and never was any bitterness in our heart even though this doctor did not listen to us, and went against her wishes. Actually he remained our main doctor, (even though we never really used him except in one situation) for many years.

With over 40 years of dealing with the medical world, with

many parishioners in the hospital, I'm sorry to say that in most situations my experience has been negative. I have seen the medical world literally kill my parishioners. I could not interfere because I do not have that authority. There is no bitterness in my heart, but just a reality of what goes on in the medical world. You see when I finally received my PhD in biblical theology, a part of my accreditation was a program they had at a local hospital.

As I went through that program, I had to just let many things go in one ear and out another. For instance when I attended this recognized accredited class back in the 90s, they were trying to influence us as clergy to get our members to sign forms that would allow them to take the organs of our parishioners if they deemed that the patient could not survive and operation.

Episiotomy: When it's needed, when it's not.
Once a routine part of childbirth, an episiotomy is now recommended only in certain cases. Here's what you need to know about the risks, benefits and recovery.

An episiotomy is an incision made in the perineum — the tissue between the vaginal opening and the anus — during childbirth. Although the procedure was once a routine part of childbirth, that's no longer the case.

The episiotomy tradition
For years, an episiotomy was thought to help prevent more extensive vaginal tears during childbirth, and heal better than a natural tear. The procedure was also thought to help preserve the muscular and connective tissue support of the pelvic floor.

Today, however, research suggests that routine episiotomies don't prevent these problems after all. Routine episiotomies are no longer recommended. Still, the procedure is sometimes needed. Your health care provider might recommend an episiotomy if your baby needs to be quickly delivered because:

Your baby's shoulder is stuck behind your pelvic bone.

Your baby has an abnormal heart rate pattern during your delivery. You need an operative vaginal delivery.

Episiotomy risks
Episiotomy recovery is uncomfortable, and sometimes the surgical incision is more extensive than a natural tear would have been. Infection is possible. For some women, an episiotomy causes pain during sex in the months after delivery.

Our Baby Michael Deathly Sick

There is much controversy when it comes to children receiving Immunization shots, or vaccinations shots. At the time when Michael received his shots, we did not think anything of it. But from personal experience we have discovered how dangerous these vaccinations shots are. Of course the medical world and the government is behind forcing these shots upon every child, even when they're just newborns.

After Michael received the shots, he became extremely sick. He could barely breathe and extremely congested. I'd have to walk the floor with him praying over him for hours. It seemed like it took months for him to recover from the shots. At that time we did not connect the dots, and he was not sick until after he received the shots.

Actually our lights did not turn on until one day when I took my first son Michael, and my second son Daniel to get boosters. My second son also had become extremely sick right after taking the shots. In both situations I had to fight the fight of faith for them to recover. Yet at that time I had not known the facts of the danger of these vaccinations.

I took my sons to the local clinic to get there boosters. As we were waiting in the waiting room I saw a pamphlet that began to talk about the shots. I could hardly believe what I was reading. On the very pamphlets the government provided it told us what the chances of damage or getting these diseases from the shots were. That particular pamphlet said that one out of every thousand who received the polio vaccination would get polio. That was completely shocking to me. I thought to myself, they are insane.

I got up very slowly, and took my two sons by their hands. I told them we are leaving boys. My next two children never had any shots, and they were never sick like my first two boys were. Our third and fourth child have been way healthier than our first two siblings.

It turns out that one of the highest crib deaths nations in the world is America. In 2016, the U.S., as a whole, registered nearly six infant deaths per 100,000 live births. These numbers compare poorly with those of other developed nations. Japan, for example, (they do not allow vaccinations at birth) has an infant mortality 2.0 deaths per 100,000 live births. The Japanese nation after allowing vaccinations, immediately seen the death rate increase among newborns.

There was such an outcry, that the government began to encourage parents to wait and to their children were two years old. Immediately the death rate among newborns fell dramatically. Actually the Japanese people are considered one of the healthiest people in the world. They're very skeptical of the vaccinations being shoved by the medical profession.

Building an Addition the Wrong Way

It became obvious that we needed to put in addition to the

church. I went to the church board and showed them preliminary plans I had drawn up. We needed more classrooms. Yes, we had a large block building that we used for children's church, and church meal gatherings. Yet, we needed classrooms for all the children were bussing in.

The addition that I wanted us to build would be 50' x 50'. Two stories, with the bathroom in the basement, which would only be 1/2 a basement. The board did not want to go into debt, and I agreed with them. I said let's do it this way. As the money comes in, and the volunteer help, let's build it.

Of course, the first step would be getting building permits in the blueprints. I encouraged the board of two men and for women to take a step of faith. They agreed to the fact that we should begin the process.

I found someone who could draw up the blueprints of this simple addition. Then I took the necessary steps to get the building permits and all that the state or the local township would require. The money began to come in for the block for the first part of this building.

One day one of the brothers in the church you owned a backhoe called me up and said: Pastor Mike how do the excavation for the basement, the footers, and the block walls. He said let's get started as soon as possible. I can be honest and say that at that moment there was a small red light inside of me. In my heart, I believe I knew that before we dug the footers in the basement I should have had another meeting with the board. But I justified in my mind the beginning of the project because we had a volunteer to do the excavation and the preparation.

So, without contacting the board, the brother came over with the backhoe in his dump truck. We staked out the location and began the project. By the following Sunday, all of the basement was dug out. Where the footers would be poured was almost ready. We put stakes up around the hole with ropes and caution signs for nobody would fall in.

I had underestimated the response from the main board member. This is the same brother who was concerned about his sons getting married to African-American girls. He really raised a stink, even though I considered him my friend. I justified my actions because we agreed to begin when we had volunteers, laborers, and money coming in. That was the beginning of the end of my time with that church. Within a couple weeks we had the footers poured, and the block walls went up. We had the money for the floor Joist and the plywood for the second floor.

The main board member and his family stopped coming to church. There was much grumbling going on in the local church family. This is where I made a major mistake. I should have stayed and finished the construction, to this project, but decided to resign.

My reasoning was that I was an outsider. If I did not have the support of the brother of the man who started the church 20 years previously, then I had no right to be there. I believed that it was the enemy that wanted me to quit based upon a wrong but sincere philosophy.

The floor Joist and plywood were placed upon the block construction. Then it was all covered with plastic to protect it. This was about 1/3 of the project. I wish I could say after I left they completed it, but it stayed that way for many years.

One day as I was going past the facility I saw that they had brought a dozer in to crush the block and to fill in this hole. The project was never the vision of the leadership of the church, but it was my vision. I had not taken the time in order to build this vision into the heart of those on the church board.

Resigned from the Three Springs Church

I was under so much condemnation because of how I went about building the addition, it got into my head and heart that I needed to resign. I put in my official resignation letter, informing them that I would be willing to continue to minister in the pulpit until they got a new pastor.

They agreed that my wife and I could stay within the parsonage until they found someone new. But it turns out that there was so much aggravation stirred up within the church board, that they did not want me in the pulpit anymore.

Because of what I went through with this church, and how it all turned out, I've learned to dig in until I hear from heaven. There is a Scripture that convicted me which says: the Hireling will flee from the flock when the wolf comes. Now, I know in my heart I was not a hireling, but I had allowed the devil to deceive me with the thought that I had no right to oversee this church because the brother of the founder of the church was the head man on the board.

I cannot change the past, but if I had to do it all over again, I would have stuck it out. I would've finished the addition, and Ministering to the congregation. We had well over 40 brand-new converts filled with the Holy Ghost. I left them in the hands of people who did not really have compassion or love for them.

The church I am now pastoring I began in 1983. Many times it felt like I should just leave, especially when we went from about 600 people down to no one but basically my family and a very small group of people. But because of what I went through back in 1981, I have stuck to my guns. If the Lord told me to leave, I would, but instead, HE has told me to stand my ground. For over

36 years I have been faithful in the church God placed me in.

As a result of enduring, we have had a global outreach to the world. We have broadcasted on our own radio stations and TV, Satellite and Internet. Owning our own 24 hour TV network (wbntv.org). Having personally helped start over 27 churches. Published over 100 books, with many more coming (the Lord willing). Started a Bible College, and Christian school. Literally thousands of video sermons on the Internet. Having written over 5000 sermon outlines on over 30 different subject matters of the Bible. Preached over 10,000 times. Having memorized over a third of the New Testament! Earned a PhD in Biblical Theology, and received a conferred Doctorate of Divinity from Life Christian University.

I believe with all my heart if I had not been faithful over the little sense 1983, I would never have accomplished by God's grace what we have up to this point.

Do Not Start a Church in Saltillo
(God does not start Churches by Splits)

Now, this is a major mistake that many ministers are making in the modern day church. I had been pastoring an Assembly of God Church in Three Springs Pennsylvania. When I resigned from this church, the board immediately decided to stop running the buses that were picking up all the children and parents that we had seen converted, and filled with the Holy Ghost. My heart was pierced because these people were left desolate.

I had made a mistake by resigning from this church. But one

wrong decision does not justify another wrong decision. I began to lean to the understanding of my mind thinking, I need to help these people. One day I was driving through a small town that was only about two miles away from the church I had been pastoring.

In the middle of this little town, that you could pass through within a count of 10, was an old high school that was sitting empty. The Saltillo Gym, which was a rather large facility, and available for rent or sale. One day as I was passing through this town, I saw it sitting empty. Immediately I pulled over into a parking spot. I got out of my car and began to walk around this building. My mind began to think about what I could do with it and turning it to a church. I knew many the people that I had led to Christ would come if I started a Church.

As I'm walking around this building I heard the Lord say to me very strongly: What Are You Doing Here? I said to the Lord: I'm looking at this building to start a new church, to bring all the people that I have led to the Lord, or were touched of God through my life. Then I heard the Lord say this so strongly in my heart it almost was audible: Don't You Bring a Reproach upon My Name!

The minute the Lord spoke this to my heart the fear of God hit me. Then he began to speak to me and he said this: many of my ministers have brought great reproach upon My Name because of building and starting churches in the same communities or areas where I had used them. It is not of me, but it is them trying to build their little empire. It is splitting the body of Christ and hurting my church. It is causing the sinners to look at my church with a look of disgust. He said this to me: the people who are in authority at the church you just left, the blood of all of those saints is on their hands because they are in authority. Once you resigned, they were no longer your responsibility.

Immediately I repented to the Lord. I said to the Lord I'm sorry

Jesus, I will not do this. I commit the keeping of all of these people's souls and lives into your hands. I know you are the answer, and I am not. Lord, first I am sorry for leaving Three Springs Assembly of God without asking you. Second I will not bring this dishonor, disgrace, or division to your church.

Many preachers are making major mistakes by starting churches in the community that they have pastored churches previously. It may even look like they are a success, but in God's eyes there not. It has never been about us, but about the will of the Father.

CHAPTER EIGHT
A Divine Download of Revelation

Most times in our life as believers and ministers we are trying to believe God for more power, more authority, and greater manifestations. In the life of Christ, it was the opposite. There was so much power, authority, Spirit manifested in his life, he knew everything he said would happen.

When you begin to walk in this realm is very important that you tiptoe. There's been a number of times in my life when I had tapped into this realm. What I said came to pass, whether I wanted to or not. Honestly! Let me share one such experience.

My wife and I were invited to minister at a woman's meeting in State College, Pennsylvania. On the way to this meeting, God began to supernaturally give me a message for this service. I have written over seven thousand sermon outlines through the years. Many of my sermons have come to me in dreams and visions. Numerous times I have simply preached what I saw myself speaking the night before from a dream I had received. All of these experiences are simply the quickening of the Spirit. We are all called as God's people to walk in His quickening.

The first Adam was a living soul, the second Adam is a quickening Spirit. In this experience, I saw a multifaceted diamond that filled the heavens. Remember, this all took place as I was driving. I was in two different places at once.

I was driving my car with my wife next to me, and at the same time, I was in another world. As I looked at this multifaceted diamond, every one of its facets was a marvelous dimension of God's nature and character. I was overwhelmed with God's awesomeness and marvelous, never-ending possibilities. I wish someone would have recorded that sermon that day as it just flowed forth from heaven through me.

They Were Hit with an Invisible Bowling Ball

When I had finished ministering the Word of God at this woman's aglow meeting, I began to operate in a precise word of knowledge. (1981)

As I spoke forth what the Spirit of God showed me by a word of knowledge, I asked all the ladies that I had spoken to by the Spirit of the Lord to step out into the center of the room. The atmosphere was **electrified by the Power of God** to heal the sick. Approximately fifteen to twenty women (maybe more) were standing in the middle of the room waiting to be ministered to. The Spirit of God told me specifically:

"Do Not Touch Them. Simply Speak My Word."

I heard this very strong within my inner man, and oh how I wish I had listened to the voice of God. Now, there was one woman who was standing in front of all the rest. They were lined up in such a way that it looked almost like bowling pins set up at the end of a bowling alley.

At that moment, un-crucified flesh rose up in me and I disobeyed God. I was not just going to speak to them, but I would lay my hands on each one and they would be healed, and wouldn't I be something (Me, Me, Me)! That's why God cannot use a lot of people —because they start thinking that they are something special. I reached out Oh so very gently touching the very first woman on the forehead with just the tip of my fingers. My wife was there, and she can testify to this story.

The minute I touched this precious lady she flew back violently. She was literally thrown back as if a mighty power had struck her. She hit the ladies right behind her. Every one of these ladies flew back like the first lady and slammed into the others. They all fail violently to the floor.

These precious ladies ended up on the floor lying on top of one another in less than three seconds. There were exposed legs sticking up in the air everywhere. I am ashamed to say that even some of their dresses were lifted above their waist with their undergarments exposed. When they all flew back it looked like a bowling ball slamming into the bowling pins as a strike.

At that very moment the Spirit of God spoke to me and said: because of your disobedience, not one of them had been healed. If I had obeyed God, every one of them would have been instantly delivered and healed. Now, instead of God being glorified, confusion had entered this meeting. I had misused and abused my position with God. To this day, I am ashamed that I didn't obey God that night. Just think if I would have listened to the Lord; those precious ladies would have all been healed instantly and God would have been glorified. I did apologize to those present.

My wife and I helped the ladies get back up and I told them I would like to pray for each one of them individually because they testified that none of them were healed. When you don't obey, there is a price to pay. Many ministers I think simply use the power of God to knock people down. But by faith, you need to direct that power of the spirit into their bodies to heal them. Kathleen and I prayed for each person but this time it was with what the bible calls "common faith" while before I had been operating in the gift of faith and healing.

(2 Samuel 24:10) And David's heart smote him after that he had numbered the people. And David said unto the LORD, I have sinned greatly in that I have done: and now, I beseech thee, O LORD, take away the iniquity of thy servant; for I have done very foolishly.

In Snow Blizzard on the Autobahn

For nine months my wife, child and I were in Germany doing missionary work. One day my wife and I with our child were going to meet some people up north. We were going to take the Audubon all the way. We would be gone for a couple days and staying with this couple that we knew. Now, we had an Audi 100 which is a German-made car. It was an older car, but seem to be reliable. As we were doing approximately 80 miles an hour, everybody was passing us.

The Audubon is a major highway that goes through Germany. Basically, there is no speed limit. As fast as you want to drive you can drive. During those days even the German police had little white and green Porsches. We actually had experience cars passing us doing well over 130 miles an hour. Some of the sports cars went so fast that it would literally cause our car to sway from the wind produced by their vehicles.

On this particular journey, it began to snow. We were not going to be arriving at this couple's house well after the sunset. The snow began to come down extremely heavy with the sun setting. I could barely see where I was going. The next thing I knew a car with its headlights on went barreling past us. Right behind that car was another car, and another car, and another car. There must've been 15 to 20 cars who were following this one madman.

Without thinking or even praying about it, as the last car in this lineup past me, I stepped on my gas. Away we went with a lineup of possibly 20 cars, following a madman. For hours we followed these people barreling through the snow in the pitch of the night.

God must've been with that man whoever he was driving in the front. If he would've gone off the road, we would've all followed him. We were in the mountains, and he could've gone off a cliff, and every one of us would've followed him.

As I look back over my life, over and over God has protected us in spite of our stupidity. We finally saw a sign for our turnoff. Thank God we left that crowd of drivers and pushed our way off the turnoff through the deep snow. We did make it to this couple's house late that night, safe and secure

Skiing in Sweden, beating Donny with ski pole

As I was in Germany, I thought it would be wonderful to go skiing in Sweden. I asked two of the brothers from the local American military base if they would like to go with me. They both agreed to go with me having some experience of skiing.

When we arrived at this particular ski resort, and we noticed that the mountain was very high. Actually, the whole thing was rather intimidating. I had skied at a local ski resort in Wisconsin, which was not anywhere near this large. After we had our ski lift tickets and rented skis, we made our way to the ski lift.

The ski lift consisted of steel cables that would take you to the top of the mountain. What you sat on was simply a straight bar with a pole attached to the cable. A person would sit on either side of this pole, holding onto it as it took you up. You would have to stand on the snow side-by-side until the T-bar was under your buttocks. Then you would basically sit down on the bar as it began to lift you off the ground.

One of these brothers that came with me was a rather tall and lanky young man. His name was Donnie. As we stood there waiting for the T-bar, I told him it was very important for him to make sure he was seated properly because we would be in the air before we knew it. The farther you got away from the original starting point, the higher you got. From all looks, it seemed that we would be hanging in the air up to 50 to 70 feet above the ground.

The next T-bar finally arrived. The minute it came to our back ends we both grabbed the middle pole. As it pulled us along, it began to lift off the ground. It became obvious that Donnie was not sitting right. He began to slide off of the T-bar. As we got about 10 to 15 feet above the ground he was just hanging on to the middle pole with his hands. He was not going be able to hold on all the way to the top.

I told him: Donnie you need to let go. You can get back on once again when you get to the bottom. He completely ignored me. He was hanging with his legs dangling below him from off of the pole.

Rapidly we were getting higher. I knew once we got to high if he fell he would break his neck or his legs, or something.

I began to yell at him: Donnie let go, Donnie let go, but he would not listen. There was only one thing I could do to help him. I'm sure those people who were down below, and right behind us on the ski lift never saw somebody do what I did. I took my ski pole with my left hand as I held on with my right and began to hit Donnie over the head with my ski pole. Not with enough force to hurt him, but to get him to let go.

We were getting higher and higher now as I continued to beat him with my pole. Finally, he let go, and down he went like a man jumping from an airplane. Thank God he landed without breaking his legs, ankle, back or neck. A little later he met me and the other brother at the top of the mountain.

He never said a word to me about what I did to him, beating him over the head with my ski pole. I think in his heart he knew I had saved his life. That is the last time though we ever went skiing together.

God Replaced A Vehicle I Destroyed

1982

One night, Kathee and I were ministering at a Full Gospel Business Men's meeting in the northern part of Pennsylvania. The Spirit of the Lord had moved in this meeting in a most wonderful way. By the time we left the meeting, it was very late. We probably should've stayed overnight in a motel, but we had a meeting to go to in the morning. So we got into our old boat of a car, started it up, and were on our way home cruising along. The trip was probably over two hours long.

About an hour into the trip, I noticed that the temperature gauge was going into the red. I was so tired from ministering and preaching I just wanted to get home and go to bed. I just kept on driving and praying. Yes, I knew better! I just kept on driving and praying. It wasn't very long before the temperature gauge was pinned, but I just kept on driving and praying.

Then the engine began to make funny noises. In my stupidity, I just kept on driving. This kept up for about a half an hour. Now the engine was making loud pinging sounds. My wife woke up and asked what was happening. I told her the engine was extremely overheated. We needed to command this car to keep running till we get home. Together we both agreed this car would get us home in the name of Jesus.

Mile after mile we kept speaking to the engine, "You will not freeze up, you will not stop running, and you will get us home!" Steam was rolling out from under the hood. I'm sure if someone had seen us that night going through their towns, they would have called the fire department.

It was a very long drive and a very long night, to say the least. We finally made it to Kathee's grandma's house where we were going to spend the night, or should say the morning. When we pulled up to grandma's house, the old engine could not handle any more, and froze up on the spot. We were so happy God had gotten us home. (I just told you all of this to tell you the rest of the story!)

We were sitting there in this car rejoicing that we had made it home when the gift of faith rose up in my heart. When I told Kathee that we need a pickup truck, she looked at me funny. I explained that our motor home/school bus is what we used to haul our tents around with, and that we still needed a pickup truck in order to haul other equipment. She looked at me and basically said okay!

I took my wife's hand and said I **would pray** and she could agree with me. I said "Lord, we would like to have a black Ford pickup truck. Lord, we need this pickup truck to have a 302 engine. And Lord, we need it to be an automatic. We also need this pickup truck to have a cap on its back so whenever we haul anything in the back, the stuff won't get wet."

When we finished **praying**, we began to praise God for the truck. (Remember prayer, supplication, with thanksgiving.) "Now thank you, Lord, for that black Ford pickup truck!" The next morning, we got up early to get ready to go to the meeting we were to be at. It was the church in Huntington, Pennsylvania, which had been a part of the tent revival we had conducted at the Huntington Fair.

We were working directly with the pastor, who was a friend of ours, to evangelizing their local community. They had grown so fast that the little building which they had been meeting in could no longer hold them. At that time, they were using our largest tent for their meetings. It would seat over five hundred people. Of course, we had no way to get to this meeting. Kathee's grandma knew our needs, so she called up one of her neighbors to see if we could use their car. Thank God! They agreed to let us use it. This car was almost brand-new.

We arrived at the tent gathering before it began. I'm sure that everybody thought that God had blessed us with a new car. We did not tell anybody at the meeting that we had to borrow this car because our vehicle was shot. I think people are too quick to tell other people what they need. I love to keep my mouth shut and watch God work.

At the end of the service, when everybody was leaving, a couple walked up to us. The husband said that during the service he had looked over at us and had a feeling inside of him that they should give us a vehicle that they owned. He had shared this with his wife and she also had a witness. He told me they felt strange coming to me because they saw that we had a very nice car. I did not tell them this was not our car.

I simply told them to obey God. I asked them when we could come and see this vehicle they felt led to give us. They informed us that they did not live very far from this meeting, and we could follow them to look at this vehicle. They thought maybe we would not even want it. I did not ask him what kind of vehicle it was. We said that we could follow them right then and there and take a peek.

After several miles, we pulled up in front of a farmhouse. There was no other vehicle sitting anywhere in sight. They told us the vehicle was behind the house next to their barn. We walked around the house and there next to the barn was a black Ford pickup truck, with a 302 engine, automatic, and with a cap.

It was exactly what we had prayed and asked God for, not even eight hours previously. Within two to three days, we were driving around in our black Ford pickup, with a 302 engine, automatic, and a cap on the back, and we did not have to pay a cent for it!

What things soever ye desire, when ye pray, believe, and ye shall have them. And when ye stand praying, forgive, if ye have ought against any: that your Father also which is in heaven may forgive you your trespasses (Mark 11:24-25).

Little Mike Has a Hernia

As you read our memoirs, you will see the ups and downs, the carnal and the **Spirit**ual, the good and the bad. In the midst of all of our mistakes, wrong decisions, and even right out disobedience to **GOD** at times, the Lord has always been there for us, and he will be there for you if you call upon him, asking for forgiveness, mercy, and help.

When my wife Kathleen and I arrived back from Germany, we discovered that our son Michael who was about 16 months old, had developed a hernia in his lower abdomen. It was later that we discovered that it was our fault.

You see, my older brother, who I lived with for a brief time in

Alaska with his wife, had told me that it was good to let babies cry a lot. When I was with him, his baby son was always crying. I could not figure out why they let him do it. He told me that it was good for his lungs.

You better be careful what you take into your heart as truth. Actually, it is not good for them. It causes them to push unnecessarily on their innards. Because I had **Believe**d what I was told, I had let Michael cry a lot. This had created a hernia. Plus aggravation for those around us. Yes, we did lay our hands upon Michael, believing that he was healed, but we did not see this manifestation. It got so bad to where we were extremely concerned about the hernia being strangulated.

A strangulated hernia occurs when the blood supply to the herniated tissue has been cut off. ... Symptoms of a strangulated hernia include pain near a hernia that gets worse very quickly and may be associated with other symptoms. If left untreated, your hernia may grow and become more painful. A portion of your intestine could become trapped in the abdominal wall. This can obstruct your bowel and cause severe pain, nausea, or constipation. ... A strangulated hernia is life-threatening and requires immediate medical care.

One morning we woke up with Michael crying hysterically, and we saw that the hernia had become much worse. I knew within my own heart that I was not walking by **Faith** in this situation. If you're not walking by **Faith**, you better do something in the natural. Immediately we rushed Michael to the Huntington Hospital.

When they examined him, they said they needed to do an operation immediately. We cried out to **GOD** that Michael would come through this operation with no complications. We thank **GOD** that in this particular situation, **GOD** was able to use the medical world to help save our son. At the retelling of this story, 40 years have come and gone. Our oldest son Michael has never had this problem again.

Over 300 prayed but not Converted

There was church which started as a result of us leading proximity a dozen Methodist young people (in their 20's) into the baptism of the **Holy Ghost** agreed to work with us in a tent meeting we were conducting in a McConnellsburg fair. One day the pastor brought a bunch of young people with him. They spread out across the carnival.

At the end of that outreach, they are gathered back at the tent to share the exciting news. They informed us that they had won over 300 people to the Lord. Now, you would think in the natural I would be excited about this information, but actually, my heart was heavy and sad. You see, they had fallen for the lie that if you had someone pray a prayer of salvation, then they were born again.

You see there is no Salvation without repentance, Godly sorrow for the sins committed, without surrendering your heart to **JESUS CHRIST** as Lord. Yet they were telling people that they were saved. When follow-up was completed on these commitments, as far as we are aware, there was not one person who ever went on to serve the Lord.

Forty years have come and gone and now this type of evangelism is worse then ever. The end results are multitudes who are convinced they are saved because they prayed a prayer. You look at these peoples lives and you see no fruit! The nine fruits of the Spirit are absent from their lives!

Beware of the False Doctrine of Easy Believism!

A well-known international couple that I knew, who came and preached for me through the years took easy **believi**sem to an extreme level. The last time they came to minister at the church where I was pastoring, they informed me about their new way of getting people saved. Yes, they were sincere but sincerely wrong. They **Believe**d that they were going to fill the corridors of heaven with new converts by this method.

They said to me: there are two kinds of people. #1 The first kind are those who are saved. #2 The second kind are those who are about to get saved.

When we went out to eat with them for lunch or supper, they would say to the waiters or waitresses. They would say: *do you know there are two kinds of people?* Of course, they would respond. No what are they?

Then they would say: **#1 The first kind are those who are saved. #2 The second kind are those who are about to get saved. Then they would ask them which kind are you?** The person would respond with either number one or they would say, I'm not sure. This older couple would say, well, let's make sure. Pray this prayer with me. The person had no choice but to pray with them. Then they would gladly tell them; You Are Now Saved!

If you were to die today, you would be in heaven because your name is written down in the Lamb's book of life. Congratulations, you are a child of **GOD**.

Then at the next meeting in our church, they would excitedly tell everybody how many people they got saved through the day by this method. For a short time, our congregation was caught up in this deception. After this couple left, I had to bring correction to the congregation. I had to inform them that there needs to be a conviction of the heart. Then the Lord draws them by his **Spirit**, and unless they make a commitment from the heart, there is no conversion.

John 6:44 No man can come to me, except the Father which hath sent me draw him: and I will raise him up at the last day.

When someone is genuinely born again by the **Spirit** of **GOD**, there will be evidence of their salvation. This is revealed to us in the Sower who sowed the word. Some fell on the road, some on shallow ground, some in the thorns, and some on good soil.

Now, realize that's the preaching of the gospel. What this couple was doing sincerely (but sincerely wrong), was not preaching the gospel. We must preach **JESUS CHRIST,** including his requirements, or it is not the gospel.

This is one reason why churches are so lukewarm and lazy in their walk with **GOD. GOD** is looking for **Believers** who are full of **Faith** and full of love for Him and others. If the fire is genuinely burning, it will be evident to everybody.

Matthew 7:16 Ye shall know them by their fruits. Do men gather grapes of thorns, or figs of thistles?..........:20 Wherefore by their fruits ye shall know them.

Pac Man Mania
1982

The Spirit indeed is willing but the flesh is weak. Now, Kathee and I have never had a TV in our house. I guess you could say it was an unspoken agreement. We never discussed it; we just simply did not have time for it. My children will tell you that they never missed it. And when we were somewhere that they did see it, it basically disgusted them.

Yet there are so many other vices in this world that can grab our hearts and mind. Now, at Mom's Pizza Shop in Huntington, she had a couple digital games. One of these games was Pac-Man. Once in a great while, I would play this game, trying to see if I could beat my previous score.

I think it was on a Saturday we were visiting the pizza shop when mom handed me a small bucket of quarters. She told me I know you like this game. Here, enjoy yourself. Well, I should've known better, but I simply gave into the flesh. I was 26 years old at this time. (1982)

Away I went quarter after quarter after quarter. Kathleen, my lovely wife, never said a word or complained as she took care of Michael. I gave myself into this obsession for the next 4 to 5 hours. Yes, 4 to 5 hours, I became wrapped up in this stupid game. In this modern-day society, that may not seem like much. The new generation spends days and nights playing nothing but games on the Internet. I guess I was a little bit ahead of my time, you might say.

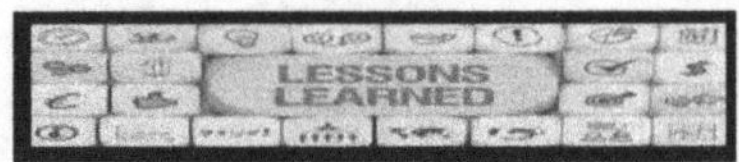

Did playing Pac-Man help me **Spirit**ually? It was the opposite. It reminds me of a story that I heard from a well-known minister. **GOD** was using him in a beautiful way to bring a move of the **Spirit**. At one of the churches, he was preaching at; he was visiting the pastor. The pastor's son was playing some kind of videogame on their TV set. He asked the pastor's son if he could join in because it was a two-person game. All-day, he played the game with the pastor's son. The pastor became aggravated by this. He said to the guest speaker: aren't you going to get ready for the church service tonight? Aren't you going to pray or read your Bible?

This is where this now well-known minister spoke up and said: no, I do not have to. The **Holy Ghost** will be there tonight just as strong as he was last night. Did the **Holy Ghost** show up? This well-known speaker said he did, but I can guarantee not near as powerful as what He would have if this guest speaker had not given himself into this foolish amusement. Do not think for a moment just because you're getting some results that you are where **GOD** wants you to be. It is so easy to be deceived by the demonic powers of this present age.

Brother Mike were you out of the will of **GOD** playing that Pac-Man game all day long? **Absolutely I was**. Was your soul in danger? I do not **Believe** that if I would've died at that moment, I would've gone to hell, but the Heavenly Father was disappointed in me that day. I wish I could say that is the only day in which He has been disappointed with me since I have been saved, but I would be deceiving myself if I **Believe**d this. Thank **GOD** for repentance, confession of sins, and the precious blood of **JESUS** that cleanses us from all sin when we confess them and repent.

1 John 1:8 If we say that we have no sin, we deceive ourselves, and the truth is not in us.9 If we confess our sins, he is Faithful and just to forgive us our sins, and to cleanse us from all unrighteousness.10 If we say that we have not sinned, we make him a liar, and his word is not in us.

Raising the dead or not

ARE WE CALLED TO PRAY FOR EVERY SICK PERSON WE MEET? DID JESUS?

Now, as **Believers**, we do have authority, but this authority operates underneath the direction of the **Holy Ghost**. The Bible does declare that they who **Believe** in **CHRIST** will be able to raise the dead. Yet, this is under the direct leading of the **Holy Ghost**. **JESUS** said every step he took was under the direction of the Heavenly Father.

John 5:19Then answered JESUS and said unto them, Verily, verily, I say unto you, The Son can do nothing of himself, but what he seeth the Father do: for what things soever he doeth, these also doeth the Son likewise.

I have had the incredible privilege of seeing amazing miracles, even people being raised from the dead. In every situation, I had heard the voice of **GOD**, telling me to do what I did. The Holy **Spirit** was leading me. There are those today who are teaching that whenever you see a problem, you can just jump right in and do something about it.

This contradicts how **JESUS** operated. From the time **JESUS** was a young boy until the end of his earthly ministry, **JESUS** walked by the man at the gate beautiful many times. During that whole time, he never healed that crippled man who had laid there most of his life. Now, if during that time, this man would have reached out to **JESUS** for help, **JESUS** would have healed him, but he did not!

This man's healing did not come until the day that Peter and John by the Holy **Spirit** perceived that this man was ready, and the time was right. That day because of that miracle, 5000 people were saved. You see, there's a time and a place for everything.

JESUS went to the pool of Bethesda, where there was a great multitude of sick people. Amazingly **JESUS** only healed one man. Why is that? Why did he not cure all of those people? Now, do not misunderstand me; if those people would have come to His meetings or reached out to him for help as he walked by, they would've been healed.

Every time someone came to **JESUS,** he healed them. But very seldom if ever did he go to someone unless he was specifically invited by the sick person or people on behalf of a sick person. The Heavenly Father spoke to the heart of **JESUS** and told him to go to this man who was laying crippled in the midst of all this multitude.

John 5:2 Now there is at Jerusalem by the sheep market a pool, which is called in the Hebrew tongue Bethesda, having five porches.3 In these lay a great multitude of impotent folk, of blind, halt, withered, waiting for the moving of the water.
4 For an angel went down at a certain season into the pool, and troubled the water: whosoever then first after the troubling of the water stepped in was made whole of whatsoever disease he had. 5 And a certain man was there, which had an infirmity thirty and eight years.

Now back to my story!

We had heard that a particular person who used to go to the

meetings of a woman minister died in the hospital. This minister who we knew personally in front of everybody jumped up on the bed and began to command this person to come back to life. Well, nothing happened.

She did not raise this person from the dead. And instead of bringing glory to **GOD**, it brought much reproach. Everybody was talking about it. Yes, I have done some radical things, but thank **GOD** I had heard from heaven. And **GOD** brought to pass that which he had spoken to my heart at the time.

Make sure you hear the voice of **JESUS** telling you to jump out of the boat at the midnight hour. By the way, that is what **Faith** is! When you hear **GOD**s voice, **GOD** will be there to help you. But if you have not heard the voice of **GOD** telling you to come, then for heaven's sake and your sake stay in the boat.

CHAPTER NINE

A Pastor Never Replaced Our Tent

I had loaned my largest canvas tent to the pastor who had worked with me in the Huntington, Pennsylvania crusade I had held in 1980. They had set it up to be used as a temporary church structure as they were building a brand-new church on the property. This new church facility was a log cabin.

I **Believe** that the building of this new church was arranged through the atheist. He had given his heart to the Lord after the Huntington fair. It was when we arrived back from Germany we discovered that this atheist (who was the treasurer over the Huntington fair) had given his heart to **JESUS CHRIST**. He then filled with the **Holy Ghost**. He had become an elder in this church, which was, to a great extent, a result of the meetings we had in the fair.

We had the incredible privilege of staying in this man's large and beautiful log cabin house. Now, he had helped the new church design and build a beautiful log cabin facility. In the midst of this facility being built, they had set my 500 person tent up to act as a temporary church on a flat farm field in front of the construction of the new church.

Late in the summer, one day, I received a phone call from the pastor of this church. He told me this story in a lighthearted way. It seemed a little bit amazing to me that he thought it was funny because it was not. He said as they were arranging the chairs on Saturday for the Sunday service, they saw in the distance a small tornado coming towards them. I do not think that they pointed to the cyclone and commanded it to stop.

From what I understand, someone simply said run. Everybody who was in the tent began to run for their lives. They said when this small tornado hit the tent, it picked up the big steel center poles like they were toothpicks. It tossed them in every direction. The chairs, instruments, book tables, canvas all went flying. By the time the tornado had left, everything was in nothing but shambles.

Thankfully the newly constructed church had not been hurt, but my 500 person Gospel Tent was destroyed. The pastor (who I had thought was a friend of mine) told me this story matter-of-factly. Then he told me goodbye and hung up the phone. He never mentioned replacing this tent or apologizing for it being destroyed. He just simply said your tent is gone, have a good day.

I never allow bitterness to come into my heart, no matter what the situation. My wife and I looked at each other with a look that said: What in the World? I told her: well, I guess they're not going to pay for it! Thank you, **JESUS**, that you supply all of our needs according to your riches in glory. To replace this particular tent with a new tent, most likely, would have cost me $10,000 or more.

What did we do? We just went on living our lives for **CHRIST**. We never said one complaining word to anybody, not even to any of the members of this church who we knew and loved.

A Number of years later this pastors marriage fell apart. He then ran off with the piano player, never to return to the ministry! The Bible says it is the little foxes that spoils the vine. We can not live with out ethics and survive.

Matthew 22:37 Jesus said unto him, Thou shalt love the Lord thy God with all thy heart, and with all thy soul, and with all thy mind.38 This is the first and great commandment.39 And the second is like unto it, Thou shalt love thy neighbour as thyself.

Called To Pastor a Messed up Church

One day we received a phone call that came through Kathleen's grandparents. It was a pastor that I had preached for in Chambersburg before we had left for Germany. To be honest, it was one of the most challenging churches I have ever preached at. It was a Word of **Faith** church that was filled with people who thought they were moving and living in **Faith**, but in reality, they were self-deceived.

James 1:22But be ye doers of the word, and not hearers only, deceiving your own selves.

What I'm sharing with you in this story is not an attack upon the congregation. Most church members will go no further than where their pastor is **Spirit**ually. When I had ministered in this church, I saw very little response to the word of **GOD**. When someone truly has a Revelation of **God's** word, The Word will move them. My wife agreed with me that it was one of the hardest churches we had ever preached in. It was like bouncing a tennis ball against a block wall. We were so glad to get out of there when I was done ministering.

Now, here it was over a year later with this pastor wanting me to come and take over his church. I told him that at this time, **GOD** was having me minister evangelistic meetings in carnivals and fairs. He asked me if I would simply seek **GOD** and pray about it? Of course, I could not tell him that I would not do this. I said yes, I would pray and ask the Lord what **GOD** wanted us to do. When I got off the phone, my wife asked me who it was and what the person wanted?

When I told her who it was and what he wanted, I saw the countenance of her face fall. She said: honey, we do not want that church! I agreed with her. But I told her we needed to still pray. We both began to pray about this situation. After a couple of days of prayer, we looked at each other, and we both said with a sad countenance: **GOD** wants us to take this church! We both knew it was going to be a mess, but we had to obey **GOD**.

I wish I could say we were wrong when it came to our feelings about the church in Chambersburg. To a great extent, it was not really the congregation's fault. They had been taught a hyper-**Faith** message to where if you used the doctors or borrowed money, you were looked down upon and ostracized. The truth of the matter is the pastor who was teaching this hyper- **Faith** message was doing those exact things he was coming against.

Personally, I do not use the medical world, but I work with people where they are at. This includes my family. When my wife tells me she needs to go to the doctors, I take her or the children. Yes, I would **Believe GOD** with her for a miracle. I have **Trust**ed

GOD for my own healings since 1975. There is no pride in this declaration; I simply had a divine Revelation of the fact that by the Stripes of **JESUS CHRIST,** I Am Healed.

How to Destroy a Church

My wife and I agreed to take this church in Chambersburg. They had just gone through a terrible split were many people had left. At one time, it was a prosperous, growing church. The pastor who preached a strong message of **Faith** and **Trust** in **GOD** had made a decision that caused the church to implode.

The church was believing **GOD** to build a new facility. They were in an old print shop at this time which they were renting. It definitely was not very glamorous, but it did the job. You could possibly hold up to 150 people in this building.

The pastor and his wife had started this church with the hope of building a prosperous and successful congregation. They had begun a building program where they made deposits into a savings account to purchase the land or the building and the land together. Now, this pastor made good money at a secular job he possessed.

He challenged the congregation to pay him the same salary that he was making at this secular job. At that time, the church was prospering, so they agreed. He quit his secular job and started receiving a salary from the church. On top of that, the church also paid all of his housing expenses. They had rented a lovely house in the community.

One day this pastor went to pick up a well-known speaker from the airport (who became a friend of mine). The car that he was driving was really in bad condition. He goes to pick up this well-known **Faith** preacher in his beat-up car. When he opened his door to let the guest speaker in, his door fell off its hinges. He was so embarrassed by this situation that after this guest speaker left, he decided he was going to buy a nice car.

The only problem is he did not **Believe** in borrowing the money. So, behind the congregation's back, he took the money from the building fund and bought himself a nice car. The second truth is that he and his family were using doctors while making it look like they were **Trust**ing **GOD**. Now, if you want to use a Doctor, there is no shame in that, but don't act like you don't, but you do. It will catch up to you.

If I ever have to use a Doctor, I could care less if people see me coming and going to the doctor's office. That is between me and **GOD**. If people want to use doctors, then we just simply work with them where they are at. Throwing away your medicine and avoiding doctors does not get you healed. It is hard to **Believe** that people do not know this, but I guess some do not.

Well, of course, when the word got out that the pastor had taken the building fund money, then on top of it made it look like they did not use the medical world, when in fact, they did, it blew up in their face. Most of the congregation left. Now, here my wife and I were in a place where we **Believe**d that **GOD** wanted us to pastor this extremely damaged congregation.

Church Full of Smokers

The previous pastor and his wife with their family had now vacated the church. They moved to another state, believing that **GOD** had a place for them to teach in a Bible college.

As we took over this approximate congregation of 40 people, it became apparent that they needed to be **Spirit**ually educated. First, the emphasis of **Faith** had been too much on the subject of materialism, confession, and not making negative statements. Dealing with the heart, character, and fruits of the **Spirit** was extremely lacking. Like I have stated repeatedly, a leader can only take people where they live.

There seemed to be no teaching on the subject of Holy Living, True Righteousness, and Obedience to the Commandments of **CHRIST**. It appeared to my wife and I that most of the adults in this church were heavy tobacco users. One of the two foremost elders owned a tobacco shop. To this day, this gentleman still has a pipe and cigarette tobacco shop in Chambersburg. There did come a time when he came, and he told me the Lord had dealt with his heart that he needed to vacate this business, but, sad to say, when push came to shove, he decided to stay with the business that he possessed.

I did not go into the pulpit and beat them with the subject of smoking. I first began to deal with the teaching of the circumcision of the heart. That the great and foremost commandment is to love **GOD** with all of our hearts, and what exactly this meant. I perceived that it was going to take long and progressive teaching, patience, gentleness, and kindness to bring them into the deeper truths of what **Faith** is. **Faith** is for the possession of the divine character, nature, personality, and attributes of **GOD**.

2 Timothy 2:24 And the servant of the Lord must not strive; but be gentle unto all men, apt to teach, patient,25 In meekness instructing those that oppose themselves; if GOD peradventure

*will give them repentance to the acknowledging of the truth;26
And that they may recover themselves out of the snare of the
devil, who are taken captive by him at his will.*

5 miles a day almost ruined my feet
(There is a Spiritual lesson to be learned in this story)
Or: Stupid Is As Stupid Does

There are so many stories in my life of dumb things that I have
done since I have been saved. So, here I am, pastoring a church in
Chambersburg, Pennsylvania. We are renting a small rancher in
Fayetteville, Pennsylvania, which was about 6 miles away from the
church.

It came into my silly head that I needed to start rerunning cross-
country. I had done this when I was in my teens. I was pretty good
at cross-country because of all the raccoon hunting that I did. Any
serious raccoon Hunter will cover a lot of ground, especially when
you have to carry the dead raccoons back with you to your car or
truck. At the same time, you might have one or two dogs on a
lease. Pushing away through the snow, tall grass, or the swamp
builds up your leg muscles. Your rifle strapped across your back.

But here I am at 28 years old (1982), thinking I could just step
back into it as if I had never left it. Now, instead of getting a nice
pair of Tennis shoes, I bought myself a pair of tennis shoes at a
yard sale. They were a little bit too tight for my feet, but I thought
no big deal. So it got into my silly head to start running 5 miles a
day with these shoes that hurt my feet.

I took my car and checked the mileage of the route that I would run. I informed my wife what I was about to do. She encouraged me to do only one mile a day until I built my body back up to that pace. Of course, what did she know? She had never run cross-country or carried almost 30 lbs. of dead raccoons on my back at times, carrying my 22 rifle, and holding onto the lease of an excited pulling Redbone coon hound. So away I went.

It was excruciating the first time I ran because my lungs and my legs were not used to it. But I kept driving myself on. It seemed like it took forever to make it 5 miles, but I finally dragged myself home. There, I said to my wife, you see, I did it! Oh yeah, I did it all right. I was having a hard time walking.

The second day came, and I did it again. This time it was way more difficult than ever; by the time I made it home, I could barely walk. Now, you would think by this time I would have enough intelligence to quit, but no, not Mike Yeager. I'm the man, and I'm going to do it no matter what.

My wife really could not **Believe** that I was doing this as she watched me in my foolishness. There was no use trying to stop me because I had made up my mind. In the name of **JESUS**, I'm going to do this. You see how stupid the human heart can be. This is not a negative confession; it is just the truth.

Psalm 38:5My wounds stink and are corrupt because of my foolishness.

Psalm 69:5O GOD, thou knowest my foolishness; and my sins are not hidden from thee.

Away I went on my third day. I could barely walk as I went out the front door. Now, you would ask me why I did not get a better pair of shoes. I think I was merely stingy and felt my feet would get used to this. The shoes were way too tight, but praise **GOD** I'm a man of **Faith**, or so I had thought.

This had nothing to do with **Faith**; this was foolishness. That third day and those 5 miles were an excruciating and long painful journey. When I finally got home, I had to drag myself through the door. Every part of the bottom of my feet hurt. That was the end of my 5 miles a day, and the end of my cross-country running.

It took me weeks to recover from that foolishness. Why would I share this with you? Because none of us are beyond being stupid and foolish, presumptuous, and arrogant. This is even true when it comes to our salvation. The devil would tell us we can live any way we want, but because we're born again, we are good to go no matter what.

I just heard a well-known minister, who I respected all these years, make a very foolish statement. He said you can go to heaven even if you're not living a holy life, and you will just miss the blessings that **GOD** has made available for you here and now. I'm sorry to say; he has been totally deceived.

Hebrews 12:14 Follow peace with all men, and holiness, without which no man shall see the Lord:

Now, I may have messed up my feet, but he is messing up people's hearts. He is telling people that they can live any way they want if they're born again, and still make it to heaven. That is the biggest wheel barrel full of horse manure that I have ever heard. Even Paul himself said that he worked out his salvation with fear and trembling. He had to beat his body lest he became a castaway.

1 Corinthians 9:26 I therefore so run, not as uncertainly; so fight I, not as one that beateth the air:27 But I keep under my body, and bring it into subjection: lest that by any means, when I have preached to others, I myself should be a castaway.

May **GOD** deliver us from deception no matter what it is. Lord open our eyes, for we can see the truth, especially when it comes to the salvation of our souls!

Touch Not God's Anointed

(Here is a lesson to be learned when dealing with messed up Preachers)   1982

So many times through the years, I have heard egotistical ministers declare Touch Not **God's** Anointed. The command to touch not **God's** anointed is found in only two places in Scripture:

"Do not touch my anointed ones; do my prophets no harm" (1 Chronicles 16:22; and Psalm 105:15).

These passages are mostly used in Pentecostal and Charismatic circles by preachers or their followers to defend themselves from criticism. Personally, in over 45 years of ministry, I have never used it for myself in any circumstance.

Of course, this helps these preachers to protect themselves from examination. It allows them to do and say anything they want. Yet they are misusing this particular declaration. Paul, the apostle himself, brought correction to the leaders of the early church. In the book of Galatians one time, Paul had to rebuke the Apostle Peter in front of all of the other leaders because he had withdrawn himself from the Gentiles when the Judizers came into a community meal.

Galatians 2:10 Only they would that we should remember the poor; the same which I also was forward to do.11 But when Peter was come to Antioch, I withstood him to the face, because he was to be blamed.12 For before that certain came from James, he did eat with the Gentiles: but when they were come, he withdrew and separated himself, fearing them which were of the circumcision.

The fact is that all **Believers** today have **Christ,** the **Anointed One** living in us. We are all set apart for the work **GOD** has given us in this world (1 John 2:20).

"Now He who establishes us with you in CHRIST and has anointed us is GOD, who also has sealed us and given us the Spirit in our hearts as a guarantee" (2 Corinthians 1:21–22).

My wife and I had taken over this church that had a lot of problems in the summer of 1982. This couple that had started the church offered to let us take the position of being the leading authority over this body. I told the pastor who was leaving that scripturally that would not be correct. That because he founded the church that he should put us on a probationary situation. I told him that he should keep an eye over this church and us, for at least a year. Then we could discuss whether or not he wanted to hand the corporation over to us.

Even though he had established us as the new pastors over this work, I told him he was still responsible before **GOD** to what happened to this small group of people. They agreed with this suggestion. After this couple left, approximately four or five months later, the building that we were meeting in was sold out from underneath us.

We took the congregation and began to meet in the local YMCA. Because all the equipment that we would need was already at the YMCA, we stored the church's stuff in the garage of the parsonage.

We began to look for a new facility that we could move into that we could call our own. Beautiful things had started to happen in the church since we had come to pastor it. More people were being added daily. We were beginning to grow and see people were being healed, delivered, saved, and filled with the **Holy Ghost**.

One day I received a phone call from the previous pastor. He told me that he was not given the position he thought that he was going to get at the Bible College where they had moved. During this time, he had not sought work because he thought they were going to hire him, even though they were never given such a commitment.

He told me that they desperately needed money. Now, he had been informed that we were no longer in the same building. I told him we were looking for a building to occupy, and at this time, we were meeting at the YMCA. He did not inquire about how the church was doing.

Out of the blue, he told me, I need you to sell all of the equipment of the church, including the chairs, PA system, overhead projector, everything involved with the church. I was quite surprised that he would ask me to do such a thing because the church was still in operation and growing.

I got very quiet within my heart, asking the Lord what I should do. I heard verily clearly the Lord say to me: You, Your Self, Personally Cannot Sell the Churches Equipment. Now please listen to this: I did not say that they could not come back and sell it. I said I could not sell it.

I told him over the phone that I could not do this for him. He got extremely upset with me, so he put his wife on the phone. I **Believe** she grabbed the phone out of his hand. She began to yell at me over the phone. She was telling me that I was not to be touching **God's** anointed.

Now, of course, I was also a minister of the gospel, and **God's Spirit** had been working through me in powerful and beautiful ways for the last 8 years. I did not bring this fact up to her what I did next shocked her. I just started laughing, not in a mocking way but gently. It just hit my funny bone that she would be screaming at me over the phone, and prophesying death, trying to put a curse or fear on me. But I had already discovered the Scripture that declares:

Isaiah 54:17 No weapon that is formed against thee shall prosper; and every tongue that shall rise against thee in

judgment thou shalt condemn. This is the heritage of the servants of the Lord, and their righteousness is of me, saith the Lord.

It was apparent that she was operating in the wrong **Spirit**, like when John and James were asking **JESUS** if they could call fire down from heaven. She finally wore herself out with her yelling and screaming prophetic nonsense at me.

When she got quiet, I told her: I did not say that you could not have this equipment and all the furnishings of the church. That is not my decision; it is yours. The way that the incorporation has been set up, you have the authority and power. The only thing I said is that I would not do it. You can come and do what you want with this equipment. I guess she had worn herself out, so she simply said okay, and hung up the phone.

I Did Not Say Anything to the Congregation

The church had already been through dramatic changes, so I perceived in my heart just to be quiet about the whole situation. If they did come, we would not miss the equipment anyways because **GOD** could always supply more.

Approximately a week later, there was a banging on my front door. There this couple stood huffing and puffing demanding the equipment. They had driven over 1200 miles. I told them there was no problem; just follow me. I went outside and walked over to the garage. I opened up the garage door for them. Then I simply turned my back on them and went back into the house.

They had rented a local U-Haul trailer to connect to their car. They backed up the trailer to the garage doors and began to load all of the equipment, chairs, tables, and everything else that we had moved out of the building where the church had been located. It took them several hours, but when they were done they drove away.

I thought that would be the last I heard of them, but that was not to be. Here this couple had done something that was not very loving or intelligent. They advertised everything that came out of the church in the local newspapers.

The following Sunday, a week after this incident, as we were gathering for the church service, one of the congregation members spoke up. They said: pastor we saw an ad for all of our equipment that came from our church in the newspaper.

I stood there quietly for a moment, praying, asking the Lord what I should say. Now, the Bible says to speak evil of no man, so I was not going to slander this couple. I quietly said yes, that this equipment was from the church with all the furnishings.

They said, what is this all about? I told them that the previous pastor and his wife were desperate for money and came back the 1200 miles and took the equipment. I said, according to the Constitution and bylaws of this church, I had no right to stop them. I did not think that they were going to sell it locally, and I am so sorry about that. I said here is our opportunity to walk in love, and to pray for that couple. I told them that sometimes people simply are mixed up in their heads, and they make wrong decisions. I said may **GOD** help all of us. Let's just pray for them right now, and give them to the Lord.

Yes, we did lose more people because of this, some people just could not release, or forgive this couple. From that time forward, we never did speak again about this, at home or at the church, or to the congregation. Over 38 years have come and gone, and I'm sorry to say that eventually, this couple left the ministry, and ended up getting a divorce. I only say that, not to be critical of them, but that we need to seek **God's** face in every decision we make.

My Dad Never Spoke to Me Again

Our family was a very closed family when it came to what was happening at home. We never told anybody about our personal affairs. I think this goes back to our German lineage. My dad spoke very little about his home life; neither did my mother. I did not even know that my dad had been through a divorce, and had married my mother until I was about 23 years old.

After I was born again when I would share my testimony, I would share just a small portion of my upbringing. I spoke way more about my shortcomings, evil ways, and shenanigans than about anyone else in my family. I did share the fact that my father was a brilliant man who worked for a company that worked for NASA. He worked on the Gemini projects and the Apollo projects. His main area of expertise was dealing with gyroscopes. Years later, he worked for a company where he maintained all of their large computer equipment.

But my dad, because he did not know **CHRIST,** of course, had some issues. He had left home at 15, just like I did. Now, he moved permanently, but mine was off and on, as I came and went with friends. His father was a heavy drinker, so he became a heavy drinker, and so did I. His father was very rough with his mother, and so was my dad with my mother at times. I would've ended up the same way if **CHRIST** had not come into my heart, and I had survived long enough to get married.

Also, I discovered the reason why we never had money was that my dad would gamble and drink it away. To what extent he gambled, I do not know because these were very private matters in our home. Now, I shared my testimony at a church service, and in this service, I spoke about the evil things I had committed before I got gloriously born again. In a passing reference, I stated that my dad was a heavy drinker at times, gambled, and at times would hit my mom. What I stated probably took less than 30 seconds to say, but it is what was used to become a permanent wall between my dad and me, until the day he died.

I had sent him a cassette tape of this message, not thinking anything about what I had said about him. When he heard what I said about him, even though what I said about me was way worse, it did not matter. He completely shut me off and cut me out of his life from that moment forward. Several years later, I went out to Wisconsin for a family reunion. He did not come to our family reunions because he had already divorced my mother. I had mentioned that I wanted to go and visit him. My younger brother Dan informed me that if I showed up, my dad was prepared to shoot me with a shotgun. I genuinely **Believe** he would've shot me.

Bitterness, hate, revenge is all works of the enemy. No matter what people say about us, do to us, how they treat us, or what they think about us, we must live in complete and total forgiveness towards them. I had shared with my dad the message of salvation, and I **Believe** he prayed a prayer to receive **CHRIST** in his life. But I can honestly say that I do not know if he's in heaven. Do not misunderstand me; I'm not saying he could not repent of bitterness and unforgiveness before he died towards me and others, I do not know.

Do not let anybody deceive you into thinking you can die with unforgiveness in your heart and still be embraced by your Heavenly Father. **JESUS** declared that if we do not forgive everyone, then the Father would not forgive us. Not only will we not be forgiven, but all of the sins we've ever committed will be placed back upon us. This should cause every one of us with fear and trembling to be examining our hearts to make sure that there is not a root of bitterness or unforgiveness in us.

Matthew 6:14 For if ye forgive men their trespasses, your heavenly Father will also forgive you:15 But if ye forgive not men their trespasses, neither will your Father forgive your trespasses.

Matthew 18:32 Then his lord, after that he had called him, said unto him, O thou wicked servant, I forgave thee all that debt, because thou desiredst me:33 Shouldest not thou also have had compassion on thy fellowservant, even as I had pity on thee? 34 And his lord was wroth, and delivered him to the tormentors, till he should pay all that was due unto him.34 And his lord was wroth, and delivered him to the tormentors, till he should pay all that was due unto him.35 So likewise shall my heavenly Father do also unto you, if ye from your hearts forgive not every one his brother their trespasses.

My Wife and a Motorcycle

After we had a near-fatal accident on our motorcycle, it came into my mind that my wife needed her own motorcycle. Eventually, I was able to find a 350 Honda. It was not too big a bike, and yet it wasn't too small.

Kathleen went through the process to get her learners permit. We would go for little rides out in the country with her following me. I had bought a child's chair for the back of my 450 Honda were Michael could sit.

One day as Kathleen was following me on her bike, we had come to a really sharp corner. I went around the sharp curve, slowly waiting for her to catch up. When she got to the curve, she was trying to downshift and was paying too much attention to her shifter. As I looked in my mirror, I saw her begin to fall over in slow-motion. She nosedived right into the asphalt. I quickly stopped my bike and parked it with Michael still in his chair.

I ran back to her and her motorcycle. She had hurt her arm, but thank **GOD** it wasn't broken. She had bruises and scratches on her hand and arm, maybe her face. Right then and there, I decided in my heart that she was not going to have her own bike. I'm not saying this decision was of **GOD**, and I simply made this decision. I did not want her to get hurt. Back in those days, it was highly unusual for women to be riding their own motorcycles. Now here it is 2022, and you see women everywhere driving even Harley-Davidson's. Maybe if it were prevalent in those days, I would not have been so quick to make this decision.

I think I simply told my wife, that's it, honey. We're selling this motorcycle before you get hurt. We put the bike up for sale, and it wasn't very long before it was sold.

How I started a Chimney Fire

Stupid Is As Stupid Does: My son Daniel was born on December 15th, 1983. This was a very cold winter. On **Christ**mas Eve we were all gathered around our **Christ**mas tree opening presents. When the presents were all unwrapped I decided to throw the wrapping paper into the fireplace. Not ever owning a fireplace before, yes I did have woodstoves, but not fireplaces, this was a dumb decision.

The fire paper immediately burst into flames, and unbeknownst to me while it was still on fire it floated up the chimney. This was a very old farmhouse, with an old-style chimney. All of the creosote which had collected through the years in that chimney exploded into flames. Instantly there was a roar they came forth.

Within a matter of minutes we heard a crash outside of our door. Now, it was a very windy and cold night. The next thing we knew to men, who had been drinking came rushing through our front door. They started yelling that we had a chimney fire. They basically pushed us out the front door, with a new born baby (Daniel) barely covered in a blanket. These two men it turns out worked for the volunteer fire department. Yes, but they had overreacted but putting us out to the severe weather.

We looked up at the chimney and saw flames coming out of the top. Within a matter of minutes there was a fire truck in our front yard. They basically kept watch of the fire, checking the perimeter of the house, and the inside to make sure that the fire did not spread. In a very short time all of the creosote had burned up within the chimney.

My wife, two-year-old son Michael, our newborn baby Daniel, and myself stood outside in the freezing weather with no coats. It is a miracle that we did not catch pneumonia from this situation. After the fire went out, they allowed us to go back into the house.

The two men who had rushed into our house were standing next to their vehicle. They had seen the flames, and over reacted because of the alcohol they were drinking. They had slammed the car into a large tree in our front yard. One of the men had actually broken his arm. Yet, in spite of all of this, **GOD** was good to us, that our house did not burned down, that none of us got sick, and we were able to return to the safety of our house. Thank you **JESUS!**

Paper burns very quickly and can easily float up the chimney. This is dangerous since flames that enter the chimney can ignite the creosote deposits in the flue. Furthermore, the hot air and pieces of burning paper can rise through the chimney and ignite flammable materials outside the home.

What can cause a chimney fire?

**Image result for chimney fires by using papers
The main culprit of chimney fires is creosote. This highly
flammable, dark brown substance coats chimney walls when
by-products of a fire (smoke, vapor, and unburned wood)
condense as they move from the hot fireplace or wood stove
into the cooler chimney.**

CHAPTER TEN
1983
Extreme Fasting Almost Killed Him
(Healing Evangelist)

There was an older brother who **GOD** was using in the ministry healing. One of the elders in our church who was a full gospel businessmen's president asked us if we would like to have him to speak for us. He was going to be in the area ministering at the full gospel businessmen in Thurmont Maryland. I said we would love to have them come and speak.

The minute I met him I knew that something was wrong with him physically. He was very skinny and emancipated. He ministered Sunday morning and then Sunday night. We did have a visitation of **GOD** during this time, but it wasn't very strong. The next day he needed a ride to the airport. I volunteered to take him to the airport because I was available.

As I drove him to BWI we began to talk about the things of **GOD**. His heart was really after seeing people healed. Numerous times along the way, I had to stop along the side of the road for him to vomit. I asked him what was going on? He said he had been fasting a lot lately. He literally was starving himself to death. I asked him why he was fasting to such an extent. He said he was fasting because he wanted to see the power of **GOD** Heal the sick.

Now, I probably was 20 years younger than him, but I had some insight into divine healing. For the last nine years, I had seen **GOD** do amazing miracles when I prayed for people. Yes, I was a man of prayer and fasting, but even more so I Was a Man of **God's Word!** What do I mean by that? I spent much time within **God's** word, meditating upon the covenant blessings and promises that **CHRIST** through his death and resurrection had made available to us.

I told this brother in meekness: brother if you don't watch it you're going to end up killing yourself. You do not have to fast to the extent that you are in order to get people healed. He asked me what I meant. I told him: brother it is by **Faith** in **CHRIST JESUS**, not just by fasting. If you hide **God's** WORD in your heart, and if you **Believe** what the Bible says, you will get more results than what you are right now. Denying yourself food alone does not move the heart of **GOD**. It is when you're full of HIS **word**, and **Faith** that you will see miracles. There is an amazing statement in the book of Galatians chapter 2 which says:

Galatians 3:5 He therefore that ministereth to you the Spirit, and worketh miracles among you, doeth he it by the works of the law, or by the hearing of Faith?

He seemed to be a very meek and humble man. He listened to me intently as we were on our way to the airport as shared with him what I knew and had experienced. When we arrived at the airport, he thanked me for my encouragement, and knowledge, wisdom on the subject of healing. We shook hands as he left my car. That's the last time I had a heard from him. I hope and pray that he took hold of what I shared. These are not my opinions, but that which is based upon **God's** word.

Elbow Deep in Sheep Poop

I was pastoring two churches back in 1982 and 1984. One of the churches was in Chambersburg Pennsylvania, and the other one was close to Gettysburg Pennsylvania. Both congregations agreed to become one fellowship. We began to look for a building that would house us that would basically be in the middle until we could build a new facility.

At that time the only place we could find was the old Cash town garage, located in Cash town Pennsylvania. The renovation of this building was quite extensive. There was only one major problem, it had no sewage system. We were not allowed to put any holding tanks in the ground, so we had to bring in some Jiffy John's, to help with this problem, but for the wintertime, this was just too cold.

My wife's stepfather was the salesman for Humus Toilets. Now, what is a humus toilet? It is a composting toilet system that uses nature's composting process to break down waste into humus, a nutrient-rich soil. Bio Let systems use oxygen powered bacteria that is already present in human waste to get nature started. There is only one major problem, it was not designed to handle up to 100 people a day. Maybe three a day!

But because my father-in-law sold these toilets, we thought we would give it a try, combined with the outside toilets. That way the elderly would not have to use the outside Jiffy Johns. Now my job as the pastor was not only to do all the regular routines of a pastor but much of the maintenance. My oldest child at this time was Michael, who was about three years old. My wife had her hands full with are new-born Daniel, and Michael, so I could not and I did not ask her to help me.

We began to have problems right away with this brand-new toilet system because people would rather use the inside commode instead of the outside Jiffy John's. My regular routine for Monday morning was to get up to pray, and then head over to our garage church and to clean up and straighten up from the Sunday service.

One of the last jobs on the list to do was to empty the humus toilet. This was not a job that I look forward to, but I had to keep my heart right. You see it always had more human waste in it than it was designed to carry. We probably would have been better off building some kind of wooden stool, with a toilet seat, and a 5-gallon bucket. Oh well, maybe next time?

On the front of this humus toilet system, there was a flap that you had to unscrew in order to pull the tray out, which would hold the decomposing human waste. It was supposed to naturally decompose. Of course, it could not do this overnight for a large group of people. I remember my 1st shocking experience of cleaning it. What a nightmare.

I began to undo the front flap when human waste started to secrete from the edges. Thank **GOD** there was no carpet in this makeshift bathroom. When human waste began to come forth, I stopped immediately. Praying about what I was going to do. This job had to be done, so I rolled up my sleeves, grab some buckets, dustpan, paper towels and whatever else I thought I might need.

I went back and undid the screws, and pulled the flap. Out came the sheep manure like a flood. Wow, what a mess, as I was scooping it up as fast as I could, putting it into five-gallon buckets. It took over an hour for me to clean up all the mess. Then I had to go home and clean up myself because I stunk. The grace of **GOD** was upon me mightily, because I never told anybody, or complained.

Every Monday this became my routine. It was always the last job I did when I went to church on Monday morning. Some Mondays were way worse than others, it all depended on the crowd, and how many chose to use the inside bathroom the day before.

On one particular Monday, after I had done my regular routines, I breathed a heavy sigh and headed to the bathroom. Rolled up my sleeves, gathering all my necessary equipment, getting down on my knees in front of the toilet. Here I go, pulling off the screws that held on the front flap with a gasket. I opened up the front flap, and out came the flood of sheep poop! Wow, we must have had a wonderful Sunday with the sheep well fed. This was always the evidence of good attendance.

Now when I tell you this story I am not exaggerating, sometimes this small 6' x 8' bathroom, would be a couple inches deep in sheep poop. So on this particular Monday, I am in the bathroom cleaning up, singing, **Oh How I Love JESUS**, over and over, just thanking **GOD** I had an opportunity to love and serve these precious people. At the same time, I would be praying for all the precious sheep who had left behind a part of their daily life with me to clean up. In my mind, I just reasoned it was natural to clean up after sheep, part of the job.

As I was singing, the bathroom door opened up. I looked up from my regular Monday job, to see one of the Elders of the church standing there. His eyes were bulging out of his head. Immediately he put his finger and his thumb to his nose, trying not to breathe in the smell of the sheep manure. He said to me with a very shocked tone: Pastor Mike What Are You Doing! I looked up at him and said with a smile on my face, Oh I'm just cleaning up after the sheep!

Never but a Humus Toilet for a community bathroom!

■ Composting toilets require attention for proper maintenance.

■ Pests and odor problems can occur if not maintained properly.

■ Improperly maintained composting toilets are unsafe and unhygienic.

■ Composting toilets are expensive compared with low-flow models; however, they are less expensive than a typical septic system installation.

A Plumber Who Would Not Listen

We had moved into an old house that we had purchased in McKnight town. Now this old house had some real issues that needed to be resolved. One of them was a main drainage pipe that was clogged. It was accessible on the outside of the house where there was located the main plug.

All that really needed to be done was a plumber snake needed to be run from the outside. If I would've had one of these plumber snakes I could've done the job in very short order. But, because I did not have a snake I caught a plumber who only lived about two blocks from me.

I told him specifically, I've got to go away so when you come make sure you only take the snake to the outside drainage pipe. There is nothing else that I need you to do. I made sure that I emphasized to him what the job was. I must've perceived in my heart that he was not going to listen. The time he had set up to come was when I was going to be away.

I told my wife: Honey when he comes show him where the plug is to the drainage pipe. Whatever you do, do not let them in the house. I had already told this man he did not need to come into my house. She said she knew exactly what I was saying. Then I left to go to do whatever business that was prearranged.

When I got home the plumber of course was already gone. I said to my wife: you did not let them in the house did you? She looked at me sheepishly and said he insisted. I said what? She said he insisted. He basically bulldozed my wife out of the way, and went into the house. Yes, I did get upset, but I did not get better.

A couple weeks later I received a large bill from him. I called him up and told him that I was not going to pay that bill in its entirety because he did the exact opposite of what I told him. The love of money is a terrible thing, and Paul said it is the root of all evil. I never heard from him again but every time he saw me he would try to avoid me. It was about five months later I found out what he had done. He actually had gone to my elders and slandered me.

Instead of my elders telling me what was going on, the church had paid the bill. I gently told the elders, that that was not the way they should have handled it. That my personal bills for my personal bills. They said they did not want the reputation of the church ruined. I said if I had done something evil, the nets understandable.

I told them that they should have come to me first before they went to use the church's money on something like this. That was the beginning of a shaking in the church I was pastoring with the elders and their wives. The devil knows how to turn molehills into mountains, especially when we do not deal with the situations upon biblical principles.

WHY PEOPLE ARE SICK & DO NOT GET HEALED!

The Title of this article actually could become a book. Some years ago I did a teaching on the reasons why people are not healed. I discovered 32 biblical reasons. For many that would seem to be too complicated and confusing. People like real quick three point answers. But in all truth life in the **Spirit** is way more complicated than that. In this particular article, I will try to just bring up some simple facts.

First we must establish the fact that all sickness and disease is from a satanic source.

Acts 10:38 How GOD anointed JESUS of Nazareth with the Holy Ghost and with power: who went about doing good, and healing all that were oppressed of the devil; for GOD was with him.

Did you notice that it says all of the people that **JESUS** healed were oppressed of the devil? Now you might say: Pastor Mike in the old covenant **GOD** sent sickness and disease to punish people! Did He Really? If you study these situations you will discover that **GOD** did not send a sickness and disease.

What Did He Do Then? He allowed the devil to bring death and destruction! Why? Because they opened the door through sin, disobedience, ignorance, unbelief by not using their authority as the seed of Abraham.

People Give Place to the Devil!

People open the door through wrong choices, unhealthy eating habits and life styles, sin, disobedience, ignorance, or by not using their authority against the devil that Christ gave them in His name. Many times, we give place to the devil because of lifestyles. Many times, we eat things that simply are destructive to our body. Yes, we can rise in **Faith** and **Believe GOD** for healing from these situations, but it would be better if we took care of the temple of **GOD**.

Sometimes I have discovered automobiles will not run right because of bad gasoline. I could pray over that car and command it to run, which will work at times, but actually, you need to put good gasoline in your car. It's the same with your physical body. Not only are people putting bad things in their body, but they are filling their minds with negative thoughts, un**god**ly images, and immorality. The Scripture very boldly declares.

LOOKING TO THE ARM OF THE FLESH

This article is simply scratching the surface of how the enemy makes people sick, and why **GOD**s people are not getting healed! I will also include some thoughts from **Smith Wigglesworth** in this article. We also discover that people who cannot get **HEALED** many times are ignorant about Scriptures. And if they're not ignorant of Scriptures, they have not **meditated** upon them sufficiently to cause them to be quickened by the **Spirit**. **Faith** is when the word of **GOD** becomes more real to you than symptoms, pain, circumstances.

Smith Wigglesworth used to always say: No Man Who Is Walking by Faith Ever Considers the Circumstances! He simply stands boldly upon the word of GOD no matter what.

Now, I am going to say something very **BOLD** but it is not to condemn you. I have found myself in the same situation.

Any Believer **who runs for the medicine cabinet or medical doctor is not operating in** Faith in CHRIST.

Do not think for a minute that staying away from doctors and not taking medicine means you're in **FAITH**, or that doing this will get you healed!

READ ON BEFORE JUMPING TO CONCLUSIONS!

At this statement, I'm sure offences will rise up in many. The purpose of this statement is not to condemn you. I have discovered in over 45 years of walking this walk of **Faith** that one of the most important things I can do is to discover where I am at **Spirit**ually.

If I am not in **FAITH**, or **God's WILL** then I need to press in and get a hold of **GOD**. Many times, when sickness, circumstances, diseases, overwhelmed me, I knew I had to go after **GOD**. In many situations, if I had not gone after **GOD**, I would have died. Most modern-day **Believers** when they are hit with a life-threatening, or even minor illnesses they immediately run to the world. It's always been my habit to run to **GOD** with all of my heart.

I work with people where they are at just like **JESUS** did. **JESUS** did not condemn them, he simply said to them: what is that you want. I ask people this similar question. If they say to me: Pastor pray that I will have an operation with no complications! I never attacked them, or put them down. Correcting people in their negative statements or lack of **Faith** is never constructive.

Our job is to bring people to a higher dimension of **Faith** and **Trust** in **GOD**. You never going to do that by attacking them. You locate where they are **Spirit**ually just like a good teacher or coach does. Then you try to take them to a higher realm. If people are not operating in **Faith**, then it is our job in meekness and gentleness to bring them to a higher dimension.

Many times, when I have prayed for people, I knew they were not operating in **Faith**. But the gift of **Faith**, healing, and miracles that **GOD** had placed within my inner man would rise up in spite of this. **JESUS** would heal them! Notice I did not say that I healed them. The operating of the gifts of the **Spirit** and the authority and power discovered in the name of **JESUS** would make them whole.

I have also discovered that many deceived **Christians** usually know only three scriptures. They know about Paul's thorn in the flesh, and that Paul told Timothy to take a little wine for his stomach's sake, and that Paul left someone sick somewhere; they forget his name, and they do not remember the name of the place and don't know where the chapter is.

Most people think they have a thorn in the flesh. The chief thing in dealing with a person who is sick is to locate their exact **Spirit**ual position. As you are ministering under the **Spirit**'s power the Lord will let you see just that which will be more helpful and most **Faith**-inspiring to them.

196

Sleeping on ice in a garage

Looking back over my life even as a **Christian**, I'm amazed at how stupid and stubborn I was at times. We had moved into this old house which needed a lot of work. There was no insulation in the walls. The windows on the first floor were all single paned. The second floor had begun to be remodeled. It did have exterior winter windows installed. The first floor also had an old garage with a dirt floor. It came into my silly head that I wanted to use a part of the garage as an extra bedroom.

The second floor which was approximately five rooms was going to be used to rent out as another house. We would turn this old two-story house into three separate living quarters. That way we could bring extra income into the house to cover our bills. Eventually when everything was completed, the second floor was rented to my brother Dan and his family. The third floor was rented to my sister Debbie.

Actually this combination helped us in a legal matter. One of our neighbors turned us in for having other family's living with us without getting proper permits. The good news is that all of our last names were Yeager. And because we were basically one family, the enforcement officer acknowledged we were within our legal rights.

Now, back to my story. Because the second and third floors were going to be used to rent out I told my wife we would have to live on the first floor even though it wasn't near as nice as the second floor. To be honest it would not have hurt us at all to have spent the winter on the second floor. That way we could have worked on the first floor, but I got the cart before the horse.

So Kathleen's and my master bedroom was half of the garage turned into a bedroom. The walls were not insulated, and the windows were single paned. I think even one of the windows was broke out which we covered with plastic. Now, that was not the only problem. The bed we had was an old waterbed. This bed did not have a heater for the water. So we piled lots, and lots of blankets on top, which we slept on top of, with blankets on top of us.

I thought that the blankets below us would keep the chill of the water from penetrating all the way to our bodies. I was completely wrong. All that cold of the water that was not heated in the waterbed seeped up through the blankets, and got into our bones. This was in 1984, and it was another extremely cold winter. How we survived without getting sick is nothing but **God's** mercy. Where our two sons were living, was also cold. But at least they had regular beds, with lots of blankets.

For the life of me I do not know how my wife ever put up with all of my shenanigans. As you continue to read my memoirs you would think that I would be getting smarter, but in many cases I even made more stupid decisions. Yes, we have seen **GOD** many times intervene, help, provide, rescue, protect, but there will come a time when the dumb things outweigh the good things, and that's when you really get in trouble.

Sleeping with Mice in the Cold Winter

As the winter progress, it seemed to get colder and colder. Now, because our bedroom was located in the garage, we did have some other guest. These other guest were the mice which had lived there for years. We saw them running across the floor many times.

One night as we were sleeping, the wind was howling, and it was so cold that we were under the blankets and shivering. We both heard a mouse running across the floor. Before we knew what was happening this mouse came up the side of our waterbed. He ducked underneath the covers, and snuggled up into the warmth of our blankets at the bottom of our feet.

Now, you would think that my wife and I would've started jumping, shaking out our blankets. But we were just too cold to get out of bed. We just simply looked at each other and acknowledged it was a mouse in our bed. I think Kathleen could've said: honey there's a mouse in her bed. I think I responded with: yes he is as cold as we are.

After this statement we just held onto each other, and went back to sleep. I think that winter we probably had more than one mouse sleeping with us in our bed. They did not bother us, and we did not bother them. Of course these mice were nothing but Littlefield mice. They were not rats or large rodents, thank **GOD** for that.

Wolf in Sheep's Clothing

Without realizing what was happening the Church we pastored was headed into stormy waters. A new man began to attend our church. He began to get close to the elders and their wives. The next thing I knew the elders began to treat my wife and me with disdain. By the time I found out what was going on, I could not prevent the enemy from splitting our church.

During this time the church had been growing to such an extent that our sanctuary was filled on Sunday morning services. Now this new man who showed up came for one reason, and that was to cause strife. Later on, we discovered the history of this particular gentleman. He went from church to church trying to stir up the stink. Turning people against the leadership. He had a long track record of splitting congregations.

This man had asked for a copy of our Constitution and bylaws. He had a special meeting with the elders, telling them that our Constitution and bylaws had made me, the pastor a dictator. That they needed to put me under their thumb. That they needed to be in charge of every aspect of the church. I'm sorry to say that the elders agreed with him.

Elders All Forsake Me

The elders called a special meeting with me as a result of their meetings with this person. The four Elders and their wives sat down at a table with me. I could tell they were out for blood! They told me that they did not like the Constitution and bylaws that I had written. I reminded them that they asked me to put together these documents. That they all had agreed upon them.

They said that they had gone over them and discovered that basically, the pastor's word was law. I told them I could see where they were coming from because I had simply copied another Word of **Faith** churches bylaws. I told them that I would agree to change these bylaws to agree with the word of **GOD** to the greatest degree we could! They basically told me that not only were they going to change the bylaws, but that they would tell me when I could preach and teach, and what I could preach and teach.

I simply put my Bible down in front of me, and I told them I would submit to the word of **GOD**. They said what? I said I would submit to the word of **GOD**. Show me in **GOD**s Word my position and I would submit to that.

At that very moment, they all began to attack me, husbands and wives. They said that I was egotistical and full of pride. During this whole terrible affair, I did not raise my voice once even though they were making terrible accusations. They accuse me of stealing money, which was ridiculous.

Everybody had agreed that I would be paid $500 a week, but up to that time I had only been receiving about $200 a week. That was my choice, which my wife and I made because as a new church we wanted the money to stay in the account to get ready for the new building and the new property.

Actually, since 1983 up to 1999 I only received $500 a week one year. Then from 1999 to this present moment of 2020, I have not cashed a paycheck from the church. I have simply **Trust**ed and **Believe**d **GOD** for our finances, and he has always met our needs. Actually, we have given way more to the church than what the local church has given to us.

When they began to accuse me I simply smiled at them. I told them that the Bible says contention only cometh by pride. I said to them who is it that is full of contention and strife in this meeting? Of course, that was like putting gasoline on the fire.

Proverbs 13:10 Only by pride cometh contention: but with the well advised is wisdom.

They must've had this planned out because all of a sudden they all stood up and declared boldly. We are out of here! I said what do you mean? They said we are quitting! Let's see how long you can keep this church together after we are gone.

I truly **Believe** that they thought that when they walked out the door, that was the end of the church, but actually, that was just the beginning. 35 years have come and gone and the Church is still going strong. Thank you, **JESUS**!

Proverbs 13:10 Only by pride cometh contention: but with the

well advised is wisdom.

Just Kept Visiting Him

One of the main Elders of our church who had left was Bill L------l. Now, Bill was a real good guy who was approximately 10 years older than me. I hated to see him leave the church simply because a man had deceived him in who he thought I was. Now, Bill was over the full Gospel business men's gathering in Thurmont, Maryland. He had me speak numerous times at this gathering. Plus we had cut firewood together and went on numerous adventures with our motorcycles.

Bill was one of these kinds of guys who had a hard time forgiving. Yet it was laid upon my heart to try to reach out to him. I knew what his work schedule was and when he would be home. I would drive over to his house which is about 5 miles away for my home in the evenings. If his vehicle was there I would park my car and go up to his house, and bring his doorbell. He would come to the door and look out the window, and when he saw that it was me he would walk away. But I was not in any way discouraged because I knew it would take some time.

There were times when I went to his house and he would be sitting out on the front porch enjoying the weather. I would pull into his driveway and when he would see that it was me he would get up off of his chair and go into the house. This continued week after week but I never got discouraged.

There are times when I went to his house and his wife Barbara was outside with him. As I would go to park my vehicle in his driveway he would go into the house but his wife would stay outside. So I would get out of my vehicle and simply go talk to her for a little bit. I never talked about what had happened with the elders, or what was happening at the church. I would just talk small talk as friends normally do. I continued this routine for numerous weeks.

One day I pulled up into his driveway and he was sitting outside with his wife. This time he did not get up to leave. I simply walked up the stairs to his porch and began to talk with him. His wife Barbara I **Believe** brought out a glass of ice-cold tea for me and Bill. We began to talk like we used to in the good old days. The wall that was between us came crumbling down.

From that moment forward until he went home to be with the Lord we were good friends. The Bible says that love covers a multitude of sins. There are times we just have to be persistent if we know that **GOD** is calling us to bring healing in a relationship in which the devil somehow divided us.

2 Timothy 2:24 And the servant of the Lord must not strive; but be gentle unto all men, apt to teach, patient, 25 in meekness instructing those that oppose themselves; if GOD peradventure will give them repentance to the acknowledging of the truth; 26 and that they may recover themselves out of the snare of the devil, who are taken captive by him at his will.

How to Live in the Miraculous!

This is a quick explanation of how to live and move in the realm of the miraculous. Seeing divine interventions of **God** is not something that just spontaneously happens because you have been born-again. There are certain biblical principles and truths that must be evident in your life. This is a very basic list of some of these truths and laws:

1. You must give **Jesus Christ** your whole **HEART**. You cannot be lackadaisical in this endeavour. Being lukewarm in your walk with **God** is repulsive to the Lord. He wants 100% commitment. **Jesus**gave His all, now it is our turn to give our all. He loved us 100%. Now we must love Him 100%.

My son, give me thine HEART, and let thine eyes observe my ways
(Proverbs 23:26).

So then because thou art lukewarm, and neither cold nor hot, I will spew thee out of my mouth (Revelation 3:16).

2.There must be a complete agreement with **God's Word**. We must be in harmony with the Lord in our attitude, actions, **Thoughts**, and deeds. Whatever the **Word** of **God** declares in the New Testament is what we whole**HEART**edly agree with.

Can two walk together, except they be agreed? (Amos 3:3).

For the eyes of the LORD run to and fro throughout the whole earth, to shew himself strong in the behalf of them whose HEART is perfect toward him (2 Chronicles 16:9).

3. Obey and do the **Word** from the **HEART**, from the simplest to the most complicated request or command.

No matter what the **Word** says to do, do it! Here are some simple examples: Lift your hands in praise, in everything give thanks, forgive instantly, gather together with the saints, and give offerings to the Lord, and so on.

I can of mine own self do nothing: as I hear, I judge: and my judgment is just; because I seek not mine own will, but the will of the Father which hath sent me (John 5:30).

4. Make **Jesus** the highest priority of your life. Everything you do, do not do it as unto men, but do it as unto **God**.

If ye then be risen with Christ, seek those things which are above, where Christ sitteth on the right hand of God. Set your affection on things above, not on things on the earth (Colossians 3:1-2).

5. Die to self! The old man says, "My will be done!" The new man says, "**God's** will be done!"

I am crucified with Christ: nevertheless I live; yet not I, but Christ liveth in me: and the life which I now live in the flesh I live by the Faith of the Son of God, who loved me, and gave himself for me (Galatians 2:20).

Now if we be dead with Christ, we believe that we shall also live with him (Romans 6:8).

6. Repent the minute you get out of **God's** will—no matter how minor, or small the sin may seem.

Revelation 3:19 As many as I love, I rebuke and chasten: be zealous therefore, and repent.

7. Take one step at a time. **God** will test you (not to do evil) to see if you will obey him. *Whatever He tells you to do: by His **Word**, by His **Spirit**, or within your conscience, do it.* He will never tell you to do something contrary to His nature or His **Word**!

For whosoever shall do the will of my Father which is in heaven, the same is my brother, and sister, and mother (Matthew 12:50).

ABOUT THE AUTHOR

Michael met and married his wonderful wife (Kathleen) in 1978. As a direct result of the Author and his wife's personal, amazing experiences with God, they have had the privilege to serve as pastors/apostles, missionaries, evangelist, broadcasters, and authors for over four decades. By Gods Divine enablement's and Grace, Doc Yeager has written over a 190 books, ministered over 10,000 Sermons, and having helped to start over 25 churches. His books are filled with hundreds of their amazing testimonies of Gods protection, provision, healing's, miracles, and answered prayers. They flow in the gifts of the Holy Spirit, teaching the Word of God, wonderful signs following and confirming God's Word.

<u>Some of the Books Written by Doc Yeager:</u>

"Living in the Realm of the Miraculous – "1 to 5 "
"I need God Cause I'm Stupid"
"The Miracles of Smith Wigglesworth"
"How Faith Comes 28 WAYS"
"Horrors of Hell, Splendors of Heaven"
"The Coming Great Awakening"
"Sinners in The Hands of an Angry GOD",
"Brain Parasite Epidemic"
"My JOURNEY to HELL" - illustrated for teenagers
"Divine Revelation of Jesus Christ"
"My Daily Meditations"
"Holy Bible of JESUS CHRIST"
"War In The Heavenlies - (Chronicles of Micah)"
"My Legal Rights to Witness"
"Why We (MUST) Gather! - 30 Biblical Reasons"
"My Incredible, Supernatural, Divine Experiences"
"How GOD Leads & Guides! - 20 Ways"
"Weapons of Our Warfare"
"How You Can Be Healed"
"Hell Is For Real"
"Heaven Is For Real"
"God Still Heals"
"God Still Provides"
"God Still Protects"
"God Still Gives Dreams & Visions"
"God Still Does Miracles"
"God Still Gives Prophetic Words"
"Life Changing Quotes of Smith Wigglesworth"